Lawnscaping

Meredith® Books
Des Moines, Iowa

Lawnscaping

**shape the
perfect landscape
around your lawn**

Lawnscaping

◄ Flowing beds of colorful perennials, trees and shrubs surround and separate outdoor living spaces carpeted with turfgrass.

Thinking outside the box

Scotts Lawnscaping is landscaping with a twist: It emphasizes the lawn. ❖ Like most landscaping books, it helps you organize the space in your yard to look lovely and to support the activities you plan to do in it. ❖ Where it differs from the pack is by showing you how to shape your landscape by shaping the lawn. ❖ A lawn can stand out—not because of sheer mass but because of design. ❖ Showcasing contemporary as well as traditional landscape design, *Scotts Lawnscaping* inspires as well as teaches by showing you how to complete projects to enhance your lawn. ❖

lawn's roots

From the smallest courtyard lawn to the vast swards that set the scene for sprawling mansions, most landscapes feature some type of turfgrass. With hundreds of grass varieties available today, one exists for almost any condition in any climate. Look around any neighborhood in America and you probably will see patches of green grass. It's hard to imagine our world without grass, but it wasn't always such a common sight. Today the concept of the lawn is well-rooted, but it took a while to catch on. One trend that continues to gather steam is the idea of the designed lawn. When viewed as a design element, the lawn becomes an essential component of a cohesive landscape. Professional landscape designers may choose to begin with the lawn and design the rest of the landscape around it.

▲ Traditional Asian gardening centered on the quest to represent natural beauty. Lawns typically mimicked miniature woodland glades.

early beginnings

Archaeologists date the origin of grasses to about 70 million years ago. Preoccupied with plants that provided nourishment, it took time for people to find a use for grass in the garden. Around 500 B.C., Persian kings began creating stylized representations of agricultural landscapes. These lavish formal gardens contained pleasure-garden carpets within the confines of courtyards. Greeks and Romans soon adopted these grassy garden rooms to their culture. Around the same time, Chinese emperors, pursuing a relationship between people and nature, developed pleasure gardens that included grass.

Some references say lawns developed as Roman soldiers spread lawn bowling games. Others insist lawns came courtesy of the flocks of sheep surrounding European country estates. Grazing kept meadow grasses closely cropped and fertilized with manure. Utilitarian herb gardens and orchards expanded to include ponds, terraces, and flower beds bordered by grasses. Gardens of the Middle Ages included grasses and wildflowers lifted from surrounding fields and set in tidy plots where royalty played games amid strolling minstrels. These parklike gardens could not be left vulnerable to the trampling of hungry livestock, so grass was shorn by scythe-wielding serfs.

King Louis XIV of France and landscape designer Andre Le Notre took the lawn to another level. In 1661 they began expanding a hunting lodge on the edge of a swamp to create the grandiose Palace of Versailles with its grand grass terrace, designated the Tapis Vert, or "Green Carpet." This broad turf corridor led guests past marble sculptures and neatly trimmed hedges. And voila, a formal lawn was formed.

In reaction to the rigid French formal style, the Landscape Gardening School was founded in England in the mid-1700s. Designers such as William Kent and Capability Brown were skilled at razing formal French-inspired terraces and parterres and designing pastoral landscapes with flowing streams, sparkling lakes, clusters of trees, and rolling lawns. Designed to be viewed, not touched, these hands-off lawns changed with the development of lawn sports such as croquet, cricket, soccer, and golf. They brought the lawn down from its lofty origins around palaces and temples and gave it to the common homeowner. Because this turf received a lot of traffic, it needed to be durable and neatly trimmed.

500 B.C.
Grass is used in Persian gardens.

100 B.C.
Grass is first used in Chinese gardens.

1159 A.D.
First written literature describing sodding (probably with a type of zoysia) appears in a Japanese gardening book titled *Satu-tei-kai*.

◀ Once covering vast acres, tallgrass prairies, such as this one in the Flint Hills of Kansas, are now dwindling remnants of the American landscape.

▼ Early Western settlers found fertile soil beneath prairies.

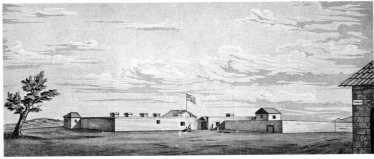

◀ Some of the earliest proponents of lawns were shepherds who found that fescues were able to recover quickly from constant grazing.

◀ Lawn grasses made the move from pastures shorn by livestock to bowling greens scythed by servants.

▲ Early American settlers imported and encouraged the growth of grasses to help contain dust in the areas they had cleared.

1299 A.D.
Southampton Old Bowling Green Club is organized, beginning an English tradition of organized lawn sports.

1320 A.D.
Records indicate that Japanese gardeners maintain lawns by regular cutting.

The grass grounds of Thomas Jefferson's Monticello were maintained by slaves who applied manure to it and scythed it once or twice a year.

A dirt-swept yard would not befit the father of the new country. Although the British style of governing was out of favor, George Washington borrowed his Mount Vernon lawn design from the English landscape.

▶ Middleton Place, near Charleston, South Carolina, was designed using the formal principles of vistas, symmetry, balance, and order used at Versailles but tempered by the gentle contours of the English landscape style.

1661 A.D.
Work begins on the Palace of Versailles for King Louis XIV of France. The grounds include the Tapis Vert (Green Carpet).

1665 A.D.
Englishman John Rea writes about the practice of sod harvesting and transplanting in his book *Flora, Ceres, and Pomona*.

coming to america

When European colonists arrived in America, they found no country manors with lush swards or fine fescue bowling greens. They faced a wilderness of forests and meadows. They set about clear-cutting trees to construct their homesteads, forts, and stockades and to open views to watch for wild animals and any potential attackers. The settlers' first planting efforts naturally concentrated on food crops. As these forts and homesteads developed into civilized towns, public areas and dooryards became muddy areas strewn with manure and trash. What these early settlers needed was something to cover the muck; something low-growing that would thrive in all climates, spread quickly, and withstand foot traffic; something that would beautify the grounds, offer sustenance for livestock, and control the erosion created by deforestation and overgrazing. Grass was the logical answer, but what kind?

European settlers longing for the familiar pasture grasses of their homeland imported grasses from Europe. One favorite, called Junegrass, due to its peak season, became so well-established in the mid-Atlantic region that it earned a new Americanized name—Kentucky bluegrass. Although mainly valued for its nutritional value for livestock, its uniform texture and bright green color garnered attention from the privileged few who were seeking landscapes to complement their grand manors.

By the mid-1700s, a few Americans could afford the labor needed to create lawns of leisure. In 1741, Henry Middleton hired an English landscape gardener to design the grounds of his plantation, Middleton Place, near Charleston, South Carolina. Although romantic arbors, azalea collections, reflecting pools, and primped bowling greens abound, the jewel of the garden is the symmetrical terraced lawn that flows from the home down to the nearby Ashley River. It took 100 slaves a decade to complete the sculpted terraces and accompanying Butterfly Lakes.

Other prominent colonists borrowed from European garden design concepts and benefited from slave labor. In the late 1700s, George Washington and Thomas Jefferson spent decades fine-tuning the gardens of their estates. At Mount Vernon, Washington included a small oval lawn just outside the front door. Beyond that, a central bowling green offered a long view from the home to the distant woods. Forty years after Jefferson's Monticello was completed, grass surrounded it. The oval-shape west lawn was the focal point and a favorite playground for resident and visiting children. The lawn and flower borders were strictly for human pleasure and sheep were kept at bay.

1786 A.D.
In Charleston, South Carolina, the South Carolina Golf Club establishes Harleston Green, the first golf course in America.

1830 A.D.
Englishman Edwin Beard Budding invents the first lawn mower.

▲ There's more to landscaping than shrubs molded into gumdrops, a 'Bradford' pear, and an obligatory rectangle of green turf.

the lawn mower and the suburbs

Among the many inventions to come out of the Industrial Revolution was the lawn mower. In 1830, an engineer named Edwin Beard Budding generated the idea after studying a cutting cylinder trimming pile on woven cloth at a textile mill. Budding mounted a similar bladed reel on a metal frame with a handle and cast-iron wheels and patented a machine remarkably similar to today's mowers. With this invention, landowners no longer needed to raise sheep or pay gardeners to scythe the grass; they just needed to be in good physical shape. Budding touted lawn mowing as an "amusing, useful, and healthy exercise" for "country gentlemen." Other inventors modified the heavy contraption to use horsepower and small steam engines. Around 1920, mowers began to be fitted with internal combustion engines still heard far and wide on weekend mornings around the globe.

The traditional lawn made accessible by Budding at the height of the Industrial Age would be cemented a century later by New York developer William Levitt. In 1947, borrowing from efficient models of turn-of-the-century mill villages, military barracks, and Tennessee Valley Authority dam project communities of the Depression era, Levitt began the phenomenon of suburbia. Using assembly-line production techniques, vast potato fields on Long Island were quickly converted into a community of row-upon-row of small, detached, single-family houses known as Levittown. For just $8,000, middle-class citizens could own a small piece of the American dream—either the original Cape Cod model or, after 1949, the modern ranch.

Homeowners attempted to personalize their homes with paint, shingles, and a few struggling shrubs and trees, but all the homes had one thing in common—the irresistible, cookie-cutter front lawn that served as an enlarged welcome mat. Levitt knew grass was the fastest, cheapest way to convert brown dirt into lush green carpets suitable for a picture-perfect neighborhood luau or a game of catch between parent and child. The image struck a chord with Americans, propelling them into the wonder years. Butted against neighbors' lawns on either side, these carpets formed continuous green strips. Each verdant plot was a symbol of unity and a source of pride for the homeowner.

1947 A.D.
Developer William Levitt uses individual lawns to link neighbors in a suburb known as Levittown, New York.

2000 A.D.
Residential lawns in America cover roughly 20 million acres, and Americans spend around $7 billion annually to maintain them.

▼ Too many homeowners, such as the owner of this house, have been lulled into complacency about their lawns.

◂◂ In 1947, developer and master publicist William Levitt expertly packaged affordable housing, wrapping each home in Levittown, New York, with a blanket of green turf.

◂ In suburbia, mowing the lawn is a right of passage for many youngsters, introducing them to adult responsibilities.

▼ Broad grassy steps and a narrow ribbon of lawn can speak volumes.

the importance of golf

Even if you aren't a golf fan, there is no denying the importance the sport has had on the contemporary American lawnscape. The game was developed in Scotland during the early 1400s, but only in the last 50 years has it directly affected residential turf. In 1912, the United States Golf Association persuaded the United States Department of Agriculture to begin researching turfgrasses and provided funding for turfgrass research at many land-grant universities. These turfgrass science programs led to an explosion of new and improved turfgrass varieties that today benefit the homeowner as well as golfers. Until the mid-1960s, the turfgrasses available for residential use were basically the same coarse,

bunching types farmers and ranchers were using to prevent erosion and to feed grazing livestock. In 1962 Scotts developed Windsor, the first patented variety of Kentucky bluegrass. Then the turf boom of the late 1960s generated hundreds of fine-textured, quick-spreading, hardy varieties that had a profound impact on the modern lawn. In the early 1950s, only two varieties of Kentucky bluegrass were available in the United States. By 1968, 38 types existed.

The game of golf not only affected grass from an empirical standpoint, but also influenced expectations. Countless modern fertilizers, weed products, and lawn gadgets advertise that you can achieve that "golf course lawn." As more men and women spend time treading the pristine green turf of these undulating, artificially sculpted landscapes searching for a small dimpled white ball, they feel inspired to copycat. If groundskeepers can manage dozens of acres of hybrid Bermudagrass fairways and 18 perfect bentgrass putting greens, lawn fanatics are confident they can maintain a perfect $^1/_4$-acre lawn. They want the professional crosshatch pattern and are willing to pay extra for mowers with special rollers to achieve it. They want the manicured lawn that will make neighbors green with envy.

◀ Golf courses have raised the bar for lawnscapers everywhere. Playing the game on verdant courses has inspired many homeowners to achieve this kind of perfection in their own lawns.

the shape
of lawns to come

▲ This small octagonal lawn has a unique shape that stops foot traffic in this fledgling garden.

Lawns don't have to prompt yawns. Used effectively, these simple green patches can be dynamic. Even a small lawn, when properly sited, creatively shaped, and neatly edged, can serve an important purpose. A little patch of grass can anchor a yard just as an area rug can unite a hodgepodge of unrelated furniture and create a cozy living room. When downsized, a lawn can actually become a focal point instead of the typical large swath that people look past to find the plants and flowers. A well-designed lawn will still highlight plantings, but it will also grab a little attention for itself.

Another major trend affecting lawn design is the desire for low maintenance. Rather than spend hours trimming and edging, why not plan for a brick mowing strip edging as in the photo above to simplify lawn care? An alternative is to pay a lawn care service to do the work for you.

The low-maintenance lawn begins with good design, which does not simply mean a smaller lawn. A shrewd plan calls for using mulches or groundcovers in areas where turf will struggle, such as beneath large trees or on slopes. Attempting to grow grass on a shady slope will inevitably lead to more maintenance. Growing

▲ Even urban rooftops are a possibility for a lush lawn. The concept of "green roofs" is a burgeoning trend.

grass on high-traffic areas will also spell trouble. If turf wears thin, replace it with a path or patio of pavers, stepping-stones, or mulch. A tree or two surrounded by grass is OK, but every tree, shrub, fence post, bird feeder pole, swing set, and other obstacle translates to a little more time spent with the string trimmer or grass edger. Dead-end niches, right angles, and sharp curves also add up to more yard time. Crisp edges are also important. Whether you have brick, metal, boards, cobbles, or a clean-cut spaded edge, maintain some type of border between your lawn and planting beds. The border will emphasize the shape of your lawn and keep grass from creeping into mulched planting areas.

Modern technology makes it easier than ever to have a first-rate lawn. The last 50 years have brought many improvements in insect- and disease-resistant grasses. The variety of grasses available means you needn't force a variety that is unsuitable for your conditions. No matter where you live, it's possible to select a turf appropriate for your climate and light conditions. Improved slow-release fertilizers provide even coverage and are more forgiving of mismeasuring and are less likely to burn grass. Products controlling weeds, insects, and diseases are more effective and selective, meaning they can be geared toward your particular problem. Mass-produced irrigation parts make it easy to deliver measured amounts of water for healthier turf. Automated, in-ground irrigation systems practically do away with this chore completely. Widely available and improved-performance mowers, aerators, power rakes, and other lawn maintenance gadgets also help with time-consuming chores.

⯈ A good lawn need not be large to supply valuable open space.

⯈ More time to sit and enjoy the lawn is an advantage of one that can be cut with a reel mower in five minutes.

◀◀ A small patch of well-maintained lawn is better than a huge, unmanageable swath.

◀ A tidy patch of turf is ideal for highlighting outdoor art.

▲ Grass is the groundcover favored by most pets. Although they can be rough on a lawn, they appreciate it as much as their owners do.

lawns as lifestyle

Lawns today are undergoing changes brought on by paradoxes. Many homeowners want a low-maintenance lawn, yet it should be perfect. A professionally designed landscape with in-ground irrigation and the best sod is desirable, but at an affordable cost. Homeowners want a lawn that is well-designed and unique, yet able to blend in with the neighbors. And finally, room enough for the kids to play ball is desired, but too much grass leads to time-consuming maintenance.

Today's homeowners want their surroundings to provide them with more than something pretty to view. They expect their landscape to custom-fit their lifestyle and provide a personal escape—as it well should. Everyone needs a resortlike setting outside to recharge mental batteries. Your landscape should offer a hint of paradise, where you can escape the troubles of the workday, a place to get you through those times between real vacations. Choose your amenities carefully to reflect your lifestyle. Do you want a pool, spa, greenhouse, or putting green? Design a garden that will beckon you outside.

Even if your passion lies in growing flowering perennials or organic fruits and vegetables, consider the value of a lawn. In addition to creating a stronger, more pleasing design that highlights your flowers or fruit trees, a lawn makes a superb staging area to park the wheelbarrow, clean tools, unload new plants, wind up hoses, or collect branches and other cuttings. Lawns have much to offer from a functional viewpoint.

Consider all family members when designing your lawn. If someone loves to cook, don't wedge a tiny charcoal grill against the house as an afterthought. Build a patio with an outdoor kitchen at the edge of the lawn. The cook can keep the steaks sizzling on the grill and still be part of the nearby action. If you don't have the budget for an outdoor kitchen just yet, put it in your plan as inspiration to save money. Planning for that dream kitchen, pond, gazebo, or other pricey feature will also help you reserve the perfect spot so that you don't have to shift things around to make room for it when you're ready to build. However, a lawn is one of the easiest landscape features to convert if you want to add something else down the road.

Children are one of the biggest factors in many families' lifestyle choices, including their lawnscapes. Provide children with their own play area blanketed with soft mulch or pea gravel to minimize the impact on the lawn. Even with a separate playground area, kids need a patch of lawn to play games or sports or just run through the sprinkler. Any fencing included should be foremost secure, but it still can add a decorative touch to your landscape. Small children love to explore their world by tasting, so before choosing plants, attain a list of poisonous plants common

in your area and make sure none are within your little ones' reach.

Remember, too, the family pet, often one of the biggest users of the lawn. Due to their size and zest for life, dogs can be tough on a lawn. If left outside for extended periods in hot weather, they often seek out a cool, protected niche for napping. It's important to provide them with such a spot and train them to use it. If not, they will undoubtedly seek a cushion of soft hostas or dig out a nest in your turf to reach the cool soil. Although not foolproof, raised beds discourage dogs from mauling plants because they aren't as likely to go to the trouble to jump into them. Fencing and trellises to contain pets can be attractive and affordable. Again, do not plant any poisonous plants within reach of your pet. Provide pets with a separate mulched area to use when nature calls and lavish them with praise when they

use it. Small dead patches of grass caused by urine damage can be quickly repaired with a handful of seed or a plug of sod, which makes this little drawback a small price to pay for the love and devotion of your pet.

▲ Elaborate playgrounds featuring plastic tubes and musical pipes are fine, but sometimes kids can exercise their imaginations better with just a small carpet of grass.

⌁ A lawn is ideal for those impromptu family picnics.

If you know your lawn is going to take substantial abuse from pets, kids, or adults, select a turf such as zoysiagrass (in the south), tall fescue (in middle latitudes), or a sports turf blend (in the north) that will better handle traffic, and plan to do a lot of aerating. Consider the compaction of a well-used lawn a sign of good design. You should be more concerned if your lawn looks uninviting and no one is using it. Every lifestyle can be enhanced with the addition of an outdoor retreat, and almost any retreat can be made better with a patch of lawn.

considering the possibilities

As tempting as it is to dive in and start digging and building, don't get out the shovel and wheelbarrow just yet. You will need a little self-discipline to get through the planning stage, and firming up your design before you start digging will save you time and money down the road. The first step is to determine your goals. What do you and your family want and need from your lawnscape? Next, walk your property with paper, pencil, and measuring tape in hand, noting existing items and taking measurements. As a last step, merge the two documents into a master plan that you can either turn over to a professional or keep on hand to work on in stages.

assessing family needs

Generating a landscape you'll be happy with for the long haul requires a little vision. You don't want to outgrow the landscape by the time it's completed. You need to ask yourself some far-reaching questions. Do you have young children riding tricycles today who tomorrow will be in-line skating and soon after that getting their first car and parking it on the lawn if you don't provide them with a parking space in the driveway? Will those same children talk you into getting a pet? Will your aging knees prefer to navigate a gently sloping lawn instead of steps? Will a spa get more use long term than a pool?

For the first round of the design process, you and your family should create a list of desirable features. Consider your gardening styles, hobbies, and other leisure activities. Write down everything everyone blurts out, no matter how silly it sounds or what your budget constraints are. Make it clear to your family that you probably won't be able to include everything in your landscape, but everything will be considered. When your wish list is complete, rank all items in terms of priority.

In addition to your wish list, you should create a needs list. Look around your yard and note trouble spots. Wouldn't it be great to have a niche to hide the trash cans and recycling bin? If you have a pool and spa, can you somehow hide the necessary storage and filter equipment? Remember things like a hidden compost bin and a storage unit for the stack of firewood to get rid of the unsightly pile of logs covered by the shocking blue tarp. There may be some debate over which category an item fits into—wish list or needs list. Do you wish you had a built-in barbecue grill, or do you need one? Do you wish you had more room for parking, or do you need it?

If you're honest about it and don't try to pass off amenities as true necessities, chances are your wish list will exceed your needs list. And, although some of the items will rank low on the priority list, they may be so inexpensive and easy to accommodate that they make the final cut. Your two lists will probably overlap each other and with a third list, which is the next phase, analyzing the site (see page 30). It's better to have things on three lists than to forget about them completely. If an item appears on all three, consider it a high priority to include in your landscape.

◥ It's difficult to sit alone at a desk and generate a plan for your dream landscape. Consult family members, neighbors, friends, magazines, and books for inspiration.

▸ You might already have an image in your head of the landscape you want to achieve. It takes a little self-discipline to delay your gratification, but take time to investigate the long-term needs of your family and the eccentricities of your site before you dig in.

▸ With careful planning and planting, you'll have more time to relax in your lawnscape.

▾ Consider your hobbies (existing and potential) when creating your landscape wish list.

◢ This rustic tepee provides structure for plantings and a fun-time haven for kids.

narrowing the lists

With wish list and needs list in hand, look for ways to combine elements. If your wish list includes a basketball court, skateboard ramp, handball wall, and radio-controlled miniature race car track, consider a sport court that can handle all of these within a tidy 35×65-foot space. If you have a small lot and would like both a white garden and an attractive entryway, make your entry garden a white garden.

Combining your lists also allows you to bring budget considerations to the forefront. Call carpenters, sod farms, landscape nurseries, and contractors for estimates. If you're serious about a particular project, most contractors will stop by and give you a free estimate. If you have friends or neighbors who recently did similar landscape projects, ask if they'd mind sharing the cost of their project, as well as any lessons they may have learned the hard way.

In addition to combining elements on your two lists, you should also search for ways to accommodate different elements over time. Perhaps you can create a small area at the edge of the patio that serves as a pea-gravel play area while kids are toddlers. As the kids grow, you can convert part of the play area into a water garden where they can cool their feet, care for fish and plants, and explore the slimy world of snails, frogs, and turtles. A few years later, you can convert the play area into parking spots for your teenagers' cars and vans.

Sample Wish List

1. Attractive entrance
2. Outdoor kitchen
3. Landscape lighting (for beauty)
4. Fire pit
5. Stone patio
6. Weed-free lawn
7. Deck
8. Vegetable garden
9. Horseshoe pit
10. Private, sunny spot to sunbathe
11. Flower cutting garden
12. Outdoor shower
13. Greenhouse
14. Swimming pool/ waterfall/spa
15. Tree house
16. Sandbox
17. Plants to attract birds
18. Fruit trees/shrubs
19. White garden
20. Sprinkler system

Sample Needs List

1. Clearly marked front entrance
2. Landscape lighting (for safety)
3. Play space for kids
4. Long lawn to play ball with dog
5. Privacy from busy street
6. Parking for teenagers
7. Tool/potting shed
8. Hidden compost bin
9. Trash-bin storage
10. Open, dry storage for firewood
11. Improved circulation from front yard to backyard

creating a field sketch

Now that you have completed your wish and needs lists, it's time to draw your plan. Unless your project is relatively small, it will help to locate a plat of your property. If you didn't receive one from a survey company when you purchased your home, you can commission one. Expect to pay several hundred dollars for a survey of a typical property. This map will show the dimensions of your home, driveway, decks, and other hardscape areas, as well as the property boundaries. If you plan to install hedges, walls, or fencing along the border of your property, it's wise to have a survey map that was certified by a civil engineer so that you can be sure of your boundaries. You can also get a government map showing the dimensions of your property at your county (or parish) courthouse, probably in the tax assessor's office. It won't have your house drawn in and you won't get the benefit of clearly marked survey stakes in your yard that a private survey would provide, but it will cost only a few dollars.

Preserve your original survey or property map and transpose the property lines onto fresh graph paper. This drawing need not be to scale. That will come later when you can concentrate better. For now, just get the proportions correct as you create a rough field sketch. You'll need graph paper, a pencil with a good eraser, and a tape measure. A compass is helpful to verify the orientation of your house to consider areas of sun and shade. Measure and draw in your home, noting any windows and doors and whether they swing out or in. Note the roof overhang and draw it as a thin dashed line. Overhangs are critical when it comes to placing plants that grow tall, as well as planning irrigation requirements. Even if you intend to remove them later, draw in all other existing hardscape elements, such as walkways, patios, decks, driveways, and bordering streets, so that you have a record of potential obstacles. Make a note of anything that needs to be demolished or moved.

Next, draw in trees, major shrubs, utility poles, and other fixed elements. For accuracy, measure their location from two established points, such as corners of the house. This is called triangulation because you form a triangle between the two fixed points and the unknown point. Use a dot to indicate the trunk of each tree and make a larger circle to indicate how wide the canopy of the tree is (the drip line).

Note anything you think is significant on this field sketch. Look at the sample checklist on page 31 for ideas, but remember every site is different. Keep an eye out for things that are unique to your property. Check with your local utility companies or in your phone book for a "Call Before You Dig" phone number. With one phone call you can have all public underground utilities on the property marked to potentially save a bundle of money and perhaps your life. You don't want to guess about electric and gas lines.

◄ After completing your wish list, it's time to face the reality of your property by generating a field sketch. It doesn't need to be a work of art, but take accurate measurements to make it complete.

▼ The best thing about modern landscape-design software is that you can easily alter your plan without redrawing it entirely. A program's ability to demonstrate how your landscape will look as it matures is also a nice feature.

◄ Note steep slopes and elements such as trees or large stones on your site analysis. This steep lawn might be a candidate for a groundcover.

A camera will also provide a more objective view. Start with an overall shot of your entire property from the street. Then take photos while approaching the home as your guests would do. You may notice that the landscaping around your mailbox needs immediate attention, or you may see a nicely planted area at the end of the driveway that needs a bench, fancy bird feeder, or some other structural focal point. Concentrate on wide shots and vignettes that will help you evaluate features around your landscape. Most people spend a lot of time looking at their landscapes from inside their homes, so take shots of the views from inside the living room, kitchen, master bedroom, sunroom, or any room that is used often. Areas just outside the home, such as front porches, screened porches, decks, terraces, and other gathering spots, also offer critical views of the landscape, so snap a few photos from these areas from several directions.

During your evaluation, remember to take photos of such elements as the columns on the front porch, convenient exterior doors, arched windows, and other particular features you like about your home. Later, you can think about ways to highlight them with plantings or mimic them with arbors, columns, arches, and other garden structures. A few detailed shots of the brick pattern used on your home, nice paving, iron railings, your favorite plants, healthy lawn areas, and other features will help you remember your assets and find opportunities to include them on your master plan.

analyzing your site

As you prepare to create your landscape's base map, you'll need to do more than take accurate measurements. You must have a discerning eye. Pretend you're visiting your property as a first-time guest. Because it can be difficult to look at your own landscape with a fresh mind, ask a friend to stroll with you to get an honest opinion of your area's assets and liabilities.

◀ Rather than dumping runoff water onto a neighbor's property via a pipe or ditch, this grassy drainage swale with a sinewy planting of agapanthus solves the problem and beautifies the landscape.

Checklist for Analyzing Your Site

Cultural Considerations
- Compass directions
- Soil fertility
- Sunny areas
- Shady areas
- Drainage problems
- Bad views to screen
- Good views to preserve or open
- Weedy lawn to restore/replace
- Good lawn areas to preserve
- Steep slopes
- Prime level spots
- Erosion problems
- Rock outcrops
- Compacted lawn areas
- Insect and disease problems
- Wind funnels
- Unhealthy trees/shrubs to prune or remove
- Utility lines/easements
- Microclimates (cold sinks, warm walls, and such)

Aesthetic Considerations
- Plants with seasonal interest
- Dead-end destinations
- Garden style matches architectural style
- Clear access to gathering spots
- Clear access to home
- Clear access to garden
- Curb appeal
- Landscape lighting safe and attractive
- Ways to connect plantings with neighbors' beds
- Color schemes
- Variety of plant textures
- Variety of hardscape materials
- A cohesive look to plantings and hardscape

Amenities
- Ample gathering spots
- Foot traffic circulation problems
- Width of walkways
- Variety of gathering spots (sun, shade, covered, open)
- Play space
- Guest parking
- Gracious entry
- Privacy where needed
- Attractive/hidden service areas

Maintenance
- Clean, easy-to-mow edging
- Multiple trees/shrubs to combine maintenance
- Foundation plantings at appropriate scale, not covering windows
- Planting for your hardiness zone
- Plants sited properly

◄ A few inexpensive supplies from an art supply store are a small investment that will help you make a clean, accurate landscape plan.

creating a base map

Armed with a field sketch and your site analysis, find a smooth, level work surface where you can create a scale drawing called a base map. A few items available at art supply stores will make the job easier. These include mechanical pencils, colored markers, a circle template with sizes ranging from $1/16$ to 2 inches, a roll of tracing paper, a "snake" (a flexible, ropelike ruler handy for drawing curves for walls, patios, paths, pools, and other free-form objects), and an engineer's scale.

An engineer's scale is the easiest way to achieve accurate measurements on your drawing. This three-sided ruler has six different measurement scales (two per side). On the 10 scale, each inch is divided into 10 equal parts, with each part representing 1 foot. If you want to create a drawing with 1 inch equaling 10 feet, use this part of the scale. On the side with the 30 scale, 1 inch is divided into 30 equal parts. Use this scale if you want a drawing with each inch translating to 30 feet on your plan. You can also interpret the 30 scale as 1 inch equaling 3 feet. Use this for a larger drawing with lots of room for details, such as a planting plan with many small clumps of perennials. The scale you use for your drawing depends on how much area you want to cover, how detailed you want to get, and the paper size you want to use. One inch equaling 10 feet is generally a good scale for the average residential landscape plan.

After you have selected your scale, draw in your property boundaries to be sure everything will fit on the paper. Next, draw in your home and any hardscape items you want to keep. Then use the circle template to draw in the trees and shrubs that will remain.

The Lowdown on Downloading

If you enjoy spending time on your computer, consider purchasing one of the many landscape-design software programs available. A computer-generated landscape plan can easily be altered and updated.

Here are a few things to consider in landscape design software programs.

• Most programs allow you to import an image of your house, giving you a three-dimensional picture of what your landscape will look like.

• If you don't own a digital camera or a scanner, many film-processing stores can take an image from regular film and save it on a disk for you to import into your computer.

• Even if you don't have a vast knowledge of plants, most programs will give you options based on features you want. Some programs even allow you to see how the plants will look in different seasons and as they will be 5, 10, or 15 years down the road.

• Some programs allow you to search a database of existing home/garden designs but don't allow you to custom-design your own.

• Prices range from $40 to $800, depending on the features. Pricier packages often offer several design programs.

• Programs typically offer from 4,000 to 8,000 plant images, paving materials, structures, and garden objects.

• Other helpful features are encyclopedias of plants and pests, cost estimators, how-to video clips, square footage calculators, project materials lists calculators, and features that show the effects of landscape lighting.

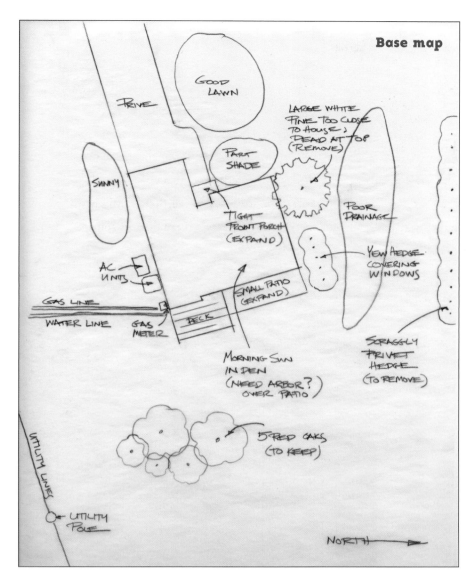

Base map

(Hand-drawn base map labels:)
GOOD LAWN
PART SHADE
DRIVE
SUNNY
LARGE WHITE PINE TOO CLOSE TO HOUSE, DEAD AT TOP (REMOVE)
POOR DRAINAGE
YEW HEDGE COVERING WINDOWS
TIGHT FRONT PORCH (EXPAND)
AC UNITS
SMALL PATIO (EXPAND)
GAS LINE
WATER LINE
GAS METER
DECK
MORNING SUN IN DEN (NEED ARBOR? OVER PATIO)
SCRAGGLY PRIVET HEDGE (TO REMOVE)
5 RED OAKS (TO KEEP)
UTILITY LINES
UTILITY POLE
NORTH

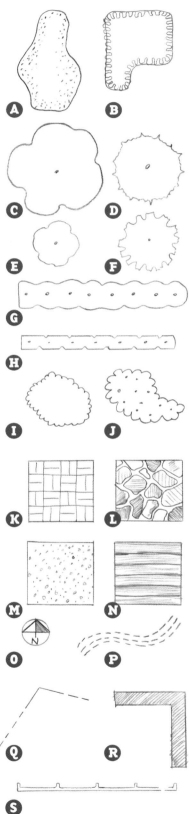

Landscape Legends

Use symbols that make sense to you when drawing
your landscape plan. Here are examples of plant and
hardscape feature symbols you might use.

A Lawn
B Groundcover
C Deciduous tree
D Evergreen tree
E Deciduous shrub
F Evergreen shrub
G Untrimmed hedge
H Trimmed hedge
I Annuals
J Perennials

K Brick paving
L Flagstone
M Gravel/concrete
N Deck
O North arrow
P Topographic lines
Q Property line
R Wall
S Fence

creating
a bubble diagram

With your base map complete, you now have an opportunity to let loose and dream up different ways you can get the most out of your landscape. This is quick thinking on paper. Get the family involved with this. The more minds you have working on it, the more ideas you'll generate and the more fun you'll have. Creating a bubble diagram is an important step in developing your master plan.

Tape your base map to a table and lay a sheet of tracing paper over it. Use colored markers and draw as quickly as you can think, labeling bubbled zones as you envision them being used—private, public, open, play, welcoming, buffer, fun, and so on. Keep it general, defining areas by use, not by future roles. For example, don't label an area "koi pond" if it doesn't yet exist; call it "contemplative" or "hobby." You'll naturally start thinking of plants you want, but it's too early for a planting plan. Don't label an area "Leyland cypress hedge" if it's not. Call it "tall buffer" for now.

Add large arrows for views you want to preserve or open up. These views can be from inside your home, as well as views from positions around your landscape. Draw dashed lines for traffic circulation patterns where people need to move from one area to another. Areas where paths intersect are nodes. Mark them with a large asterisk. These are prime candidates for entrance arbors, benches, or small patios on your master plan. Note any edges with a zigzag line on your bubble diagram. Use a thick zigzag for edges that are hard and real, such as a highway or creek, and use a thin zigzag for edges that are soft and virtually invisible, such as where your lawn ends and a neighbor's begins. Views,

nodes, and edges can help you decide where to place bubbles. Consider a buffer bubble near a busy street edge to give yourself privacy. Include a welcoming bubble with an accompanying view arrow in the same spot to consider adding a place where you could sit and people-watch or greet passing neighbors. Tracing paper is inexpensive, so just keep rolling it out, laying down your first impressions and exploring different options.

As you draw, think about how the different zones relate to each other and to your home. For example, the gracious bubble might work best surrounded by the home, the welcoming bubble, and the fun bubble, because all four things relate to each other. On the other hand, the quiet contemplation bubble relates better to the privacy buffer bubble and the nature-appreciation bubble, so work on placing them near each other. Hopefully, some patterns will emerge and bubbles will start to feel right in certain spots. This is the evolution of your design.

▲ Mentally put aside your wants and needs while generating bubble diagrams.

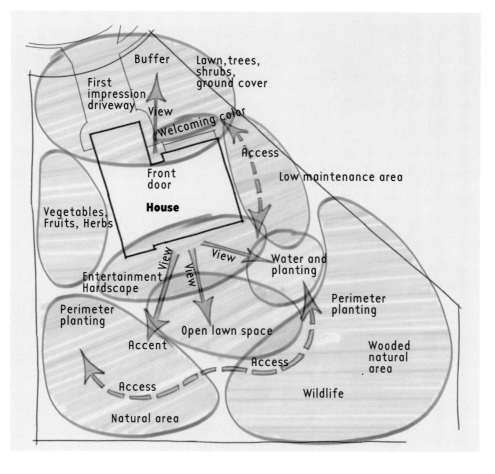

Seeking Professional Help

Whether you just want to bounce your ideas off someone or you prefer to leave the master planning to a professional, you have a number of options when it comes to hiring help. Always ask pros to bring a portfolio of their work and then check their references.

• Landscape architects generally have a degree in landscape architecture. In most states, they must pass a rigorous licensing exam. If you're calling blindly from the phone book, your first question should be whether they do residential design. They may or may not be members of the American Society of Landscape Architects (ASLA), a professional organization unrelated to the state licensing boards.

• Landscape designers usually specialize in residential landscape design. They may not have any formal education, so be sure to inquire about their training. If they belong to the Association of Professional Landscape Designers (APLD), this is a good sign they are skilled and are committed to the landscape design profession.

• Horticulturists and garden designers tend to be plant focused. Many have a degree in horticulture. Often, garden centers employ horticulturists and garden designers who can help you with a landscape plan. The service may be free if you agree to purchase your plants from them or allow them to do the installation. Naturally, they are going to limit your planting scheme and projects to plants they stock and projects they are capable of doing.

• Landscape contractors have many different specialties, but they are usually focused on constructing hardscape elements such as walls, patios, driveways, and arbors. A contractor may employ crews with different skills, such as pool construction, brick and stone masonry, and carpentry. A contractor should be licensed by the state licensing board and be able to provide you a state contractor's number. Membership in the Associated Landscpe Contractors of America is an indication the contractor is not a fly-by-night operation. Check that the contractor is bonded and insured before crews begin work on your landscape project.

▲ Consider consulting a local landscape architect or designer to check your landscape plan. That person may be able to point out potential trouble spots or suggest plants and materials with which you may not be familiar.

the landscape plan

The next step is to combine your wants and needs lists, your site analysis, and your bubble diagram to generate a master plan. Consider this a process. Rather than sitting down to generate a single, perfect plan, think through a number of options that suit your needs.

Even if you're feeling confident enough to create a detailed master plan, you should still preserve your base map and lay tracing paper or vellum on top of it to draw your final plan. You may make mistakes or change your mind and want to start over. Although tracing paper feels flimsy, it actually holds up well over time and is easy to color with markers if you want to give your plan a finished appearance that's easier to read. Using a pencil with thick, dark lead, trace your property lines, your house, and any hardscape elements that are going to stay put.

Now it's time to get the creative juices flowing and start designing the things that, before now, existed only in your imagination. Many designers begin by drawing in the hardscape elements, then outlining the beds and labeling everything that remains as lawn. However, your landscape will be more cohesive if you reverse this process or design all of these elements simultaneously. Obviously something needs to be drawn first, but try to resist making firm lines for any of the features as you sketch a solution. Try different shapes for lawn areas, decks, patios, and other garden rooms. Play with different configurations for paths, walls, and edges of beds.

If you haven't already, do some research so that you can decide which materials you will want to use—stone, brick, gravel, concrete, decking, or other material. If you haven't decided exactly what materials you'll be using, outline paved areas but wait to draw in a surface texture. The same holds true for plants. You can use the same symbols you used on your base map and label areas "lawn," "evergreen groundcover," "evergreen hedge," and so on. Then add the names of specific varieties later, after a visit to the sod farm or the nursery. Some designers choose to do a detailed planting plan as a separate drawing after they have all the elements in place on the master plan. If you're using tracing paper, this is easy to do, because you can just lay it on top. It gives you more flexibility if you change your mind after you spot a new plant at the nursery or in a catalog, magazine, book, or a friend's yard.

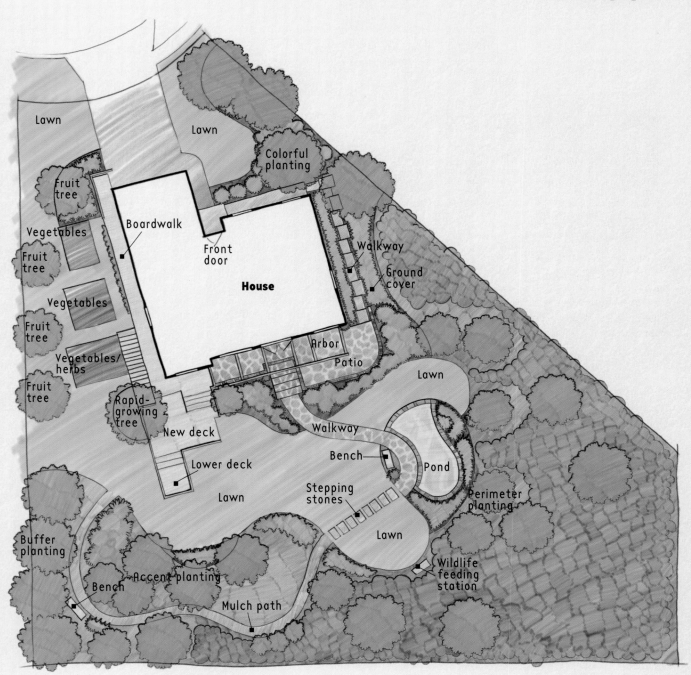

Lawn

Lawn

Colorful planting

Fruit tree

Vegetables

Fruit tree

Boardwalk

Front door

Walkway

Ground cover

Vegetables

House

Fruit tree

Vegetables/ herbs

Arbor

Patio

Lawn

Fruit tree

Rapid-growing tree

New deck

Walkway

Pond

Lower deck

Bench

Stepping stones

Perimeter planting

Lawn

Lawn

Buffer planting

Wildlife feeding station

Bench

Accent planting

Mulch path

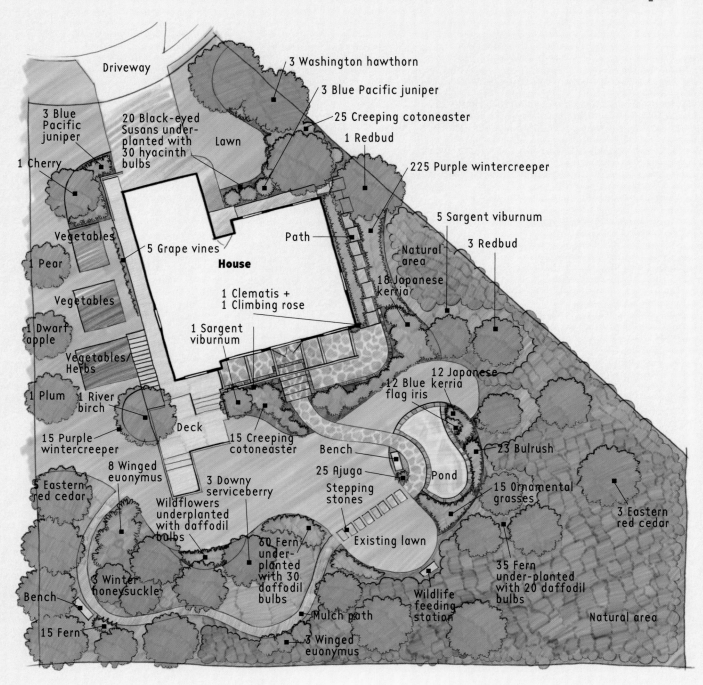

3 Washington hawthorn

3 Blue Pacific juniper

25 Creeping cotoneaster

Driveway

3 Blue Pacific juniper

1 Redbud

20 Black-eyed Susans under-planted with 30 hyacinth bulbs

Lawn

225 Purple wintercreeper

1 Cherry

5 Sargent viburnum

3 Redbud

Vegetables

Path

5 Grape vines

House

Natural area

1 Pear

18 Japanese kerria

Vegetables

1 Clematis + 1 Climbing rose

1 Dwarf apple

1 Sargent viburnum

Vegetables/ Herbs

12 Japanese kerria

1 Plum   1 River birch

12 Blue flag iris

15 Creeping cotoneaster

Bench

23 Bulrush

15 Purple wintercreeper

Deck

25 Ajuga

Pond

15 Ornamental grasses

8 Winged euonymus

3 Downy serviceberry

Stepping stones

3 Eastern red cedar

5 Eastern red cedar

Wildflowers underplanted with daffodil bulbs

Existing lawn

35 Fern under-planted with 20 daffodil bulbs

60 Fern under-planted with 30 daffodil bulbs

3 Winter honeysuckle

Wildlife feeding station

Natural area

Bench

Mulch path

15 Fern

3 Winged euonymus

creating a master plan

After going through half a roll of tracing paper, you hopefully have generated some solutions and made some decisions about the placement of landscape elements, surface materials, and plants. Create one final drawing to crystallize all your thoughts and help you get firm estimates from contractors or actual prices from nurseries, sod farms, and stone yards. If you know you will need to fill a 40×50-foot space with lawn, a garden center should be able to tell you exactly what it will cost to seed or sod. The same goes for a price from the stone yard if you want a slate walkway that's 3 feet wide and 20 feet long. Always double-check your measurements (with the tape measure in the yard, as well as with the engineer's scale on your drawing) before ordering materials.

If you have room on your master plan to start specifying plants, go ahead. If the master plan is starting to look cluttered, put plant names on a separate planting plan. You probably have a few favorite plants that you know you want to use in your landscape. If you still have some plants to select or you aren't sure the location you have

picked out for your old favorites suits their requirements for sun, soil, water, and other environmental conditions, visit a good local nursery. Actually visit several to see what all your options are. Keep an open mind and be willing to accept some substitutes and adjust bed lines, but don't compromise all of your selections just because one nursery doesn't stock the plants you're seeking. You can also shop via the Internet or mail-order catalogs if you don't mind waiting. In most areas of the United States, nurseries won't field-dig trees and shrubs during summer, so you'll have to wait until fall or substitute container-grown plants. Even if the container-grown plants are slightly smaller than you envisioned, they typically establish themselves quickly because all their roots are intact, unlike field-dug plants.

At this point, you may want to call in a professional landscape architect or designer for a quick consultation. Most residential landscape professionals have a standard per-hour consultation fee and are willing to stop by and offer suggestions on how you could alter your plan or on possible substitutions for plants. They can recommend contractors who build decks, install masonry walls, or do other construction beyond your capabilities. You could also hire them to finalize your plan or draw construction details for arbors, decks, and other projects that you can either use as a guide to build yourself or pass along to a contractor to clarify the materials or quality of construction you want.

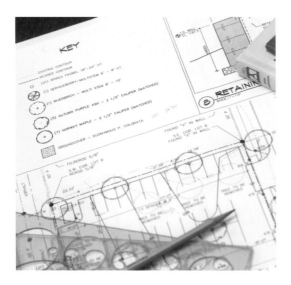

◄ A landscape architect can offer construction details for complicated projects such as a retaining wall.

living in your lawnscape

Everyone needs a special garden place that provides some of the comforts of home yet allows open access to the sights, sounds, smells, and textures of nature. ⫿ To create these special places, think of your lawnscape as a series of outdoor rooms with outside-versions of floors, walls, and ceilings. ⫿ Some rooms are straightforward, with a floor of flagstone, four stucco walls, and a ceiling fashioned from a cedar arbor. ⫿ Others require a little imagination to discern the floor of wild grasses and wildflowers, walls of trees and an expanding horizon, and a ceiling of sky. ⫿

benefits of
a living carpet

Paving, decking, and groundcovers can make up a floor in a garden room, but if you want to quickly and inexpensively cover a large expanse of ground with something natural, soft, colorful, and inviting, grass is the obvious answer. With approximately 24 million acres of grass covering residential lawns in the United States, it's by far the most popular material for covering outdoor floors. That's because grass is not just a pretty face. It has beauty and toughness.

Like early settlers whose log houses were surrounded by muck, today's owners of newly constructed homes know how important it is to cover bare soil as soon as the last subcontractor pulls out of the yard. The network of grass roots holds precious topsoil in place and prevents mud from being tracked onto the new floors. Neighbors will appreciate your effort to beautify the community. The real estate agent's favorite expression, "curb appeal," is nearly synonymous with "nice lawn." A healthy landscape adds as much as 15 percent to the value of a home.

Other benefits of a lawn include its ability to soften noise, filter pollutants, produce oxygen, and lower the temperature around a home. Traffic, power lawn equipment, construction, and other noises that assault the eardrums are reverberated by homes and hardscape, such as driveways and patios. Grass absorbs and disperses sound waves, especially when combined with other plants.

When it comes to environmental contributions, grass is an unsung hero. Research has shown that it absorbs hundreds of pounds of pollutants from the air and water each year. Sulfur dioxide, nitrogen dioxide, hydrogen fluoride, nitrates, lead, and other toxins released by factories and automobiles are filtered by lawns before they contaminate streams, ponds, lakes, rivers, and groundwater. Grass is equally effective at trapping airborne dust and returning it to the soil.

As you probably learned in grade-school science class, plants have the amazing ability to take in the carbon dioxide humans breathe out and convert it to oxygen. What your teacher may not have told you is that grass is even more efficient at this process than trees. An average residential lawn of 5,000 square feet produces enough oxygen daily to sustain eight people. It would take two 100-foot-tall trees to produce the same amount of oxygen. Grass also has a tremendous cooling effect on the environment. When the temperature on your driveway reaches 100 degrees, your lawn's temperature will be a comfortable 70 degrees. Add a few shade trees overhead, and you practically have outdoor air-conditioning.

Environmental benefits aside, turf is tough enough to withstand a brutal neighborhood soccer match, constant lawn tractor traffic, and the onslaught of millions of pests that want a piece of it. Yet it's soft enough to serve as a blanket for a backyard picnic, to cushion a game-saving diving catch in center field, and to visually temper a home's hardscape. No wonder so many people select grass for their outdoor living carpet.

⤒ A compact lawn in an outdoor room serves the same purpose as an area rug in an indoor living room or den.

◥ Turn a small space to your advantage when building a garden room. A gracious entry, fence, raised planter, and brick paths lend a homey feel to this cozy backyard.

◥ A lush lawn might bring back memories of the shag carpet of the '70s.

▶ Sod is easier to lay in a yard than carpet in a home.

getting to know lawn grasses

From across the street, all turfgrasses look pretty much the same. However, many different grasses are suitable for lawns. Knowing the individual types of turf will help you select the best one for your lawnscape.

Grasses are categorized as warm season or cool season based on where and how they grow. Warm-season grasses prefer the long, hot summers of southern regions, and cool-season grasses grow best in northern regions, where summer temperatures get hot but not for very long. The type of grass you have determines when to plant, fertilize, aerate, and overseed, all of which are usually best done just before or during the time when a grass is at its growth peak.

Cool-season grasses grow actively during spring and fall, when temperatures range from 65 to 75 degrees. As summer temperatures reach the 90s, these grasses grow more slowly and may turn brown and go dormant if hot, dry weather persists. They require frequent irrigation to keep them green through summer. They will perk up again when relief comes from the cooler temperatures and the rains of fall. They may lose their fresh spring green color during winter or turn brown and go dormant in colder regions.

Warm-season grasses green up slowly in spring and hit their stride during the heat of summer. They look their best when temperatures are consistently between 80 and 95 degrees. When fall frosts arrive, they go dormant and turn brown. If brown isn't your color, this is the time to overseed with cool-season grasses such as rough bluegrass or perennial ryegrass to achieve a carpet of green through the winter. After the weather warms up in midspring, the cool-season grasses will die. This is the time to aerate, fertilize, and plant warm-season grasses.

Turfgrasses are also categorized by how they grow—spreading or bunching. Spreading grasses grow via stolons or rhizomes, which are stems that grow horizontally along the ground or just under the surface. As they sprawl, they send roots down and blades up at intervals along their lengths. Centipedegrass, zoysiagrass, Kentucky bluegrass, Bermudagrass, St. Augustinegrass, creeping fescue, and bentgrass are members of this group. Because spreading grasses form a thick mat of roots, stolons, and rhizomes, they lend themselves well to sod production. With regular feeding they can easily fill in thin spots in your lawn. Bunching grasses grow in tufts, which makes them likely candidates for seeding. Ryegrass and tall, hard, chewings, and sheep fescue are bunchgrasses.

The last way to classify grasses is by texture—from fine to coarse. Besides appearance, texture also correlates with maintenance levels. On the fine-textured end are fine fescue, bentgrass, 'Tifway' Bermudagrass, Kentucky bluegrass, and 'Emerald' zoysiagrass. These refined grasses are highly prized, but they also are higher maintenance in terms of fertilization, irrigation, aeration, dethatching, and insect and disease control. Buffalograss is a rare exception. This fine-textured turf requires almost no maintenance, but then it won't give a grass connoisseur that thick green, pristine appearance expected of other fine-blade grasses. Coarse-texture grasses include St. Augustinegrass, tall fescue, 'Meyer' zoysiagrass, and Bahiagrass. Although these grasses are not refined in appearance, they do have strong suits. Coarse grasses tend to be lower maintenance. Medium-texture grasses, such as Bermudagrass, centipedegrass, and perennial ryegrass, tend to get by with a moderate amount of care and provide an adequate lawn that looks satisfactory to the average lawn owner.

▲ The entrance to a garden room is critical. A clearly defined arbor entrance, lawn foyer, and inviting bench make this alfresco parlor a success.

◄ Bricks, stones, and other hardscape serve best for high-traffic garden rooms. For a private escape for one person or two, however, consider the advantages of a surface made of lush lawn.

grasses up close and personal

Whether you're starting a new lawn or nursing an existing one, you should know a little about the common varieties of turf and their care. You may be able to determine the type of grass you have by visiting the Scotts web site at www.scotts.com and clicking on the "Identify Your Grass" tool. If you have doubts about the type of grass you have, take a sample to your local extension agent for a positive identification. Many fertilizers and selective herbicides can prove deadly for certain grass varieties, so it's important to know what you type have. Several common turfgrasses are described here.

fescues (*Festuca* spp.)

Fescues are cool-season grasses that range from fine-texture lawn grasses found in the highest quality turf areas to coarse bunching grasses that belong in a pasture. Red fescue, chewings fescue, hard fescue, and sheep fescue are all fine-textured. As European natives, fine fescues are well-adapted to cool, moist climates. They are also valued for their shade tolerance. Blends of improved cultivars have better insect tolerance and more heat and cold hardiness, but fine fescues still perform best in the northeastern and northwestern United States. Fine fescues are often found in shade mixtures, which contain different species of grasses. (Blends contain a mix of different cultivars from the same species.) Tall fescue is a coarse bunching grass. It is not as cold tolerant as fine fescue, but it offers greater tolerance for heat, drought, and heavy traffic. It is a good cool-season grass for the northern part of southern regions.

zoysiagrass (*Zoysia japonica*)

Popular in the South, this warm-season grass thrives in poor soils, drought, and medium traffic. It prefers full sun but tolerates light shade. The stiff, needlelike blade tips make a barefoot stroll on the lawn like walking on brush bristles. The finer-textured 'Emerald' zoysiagrass is a softer solution to this problem. Zoysiagrass spreads rapidly from plugs, an inexpensive method of establishment, and is commonly grown by sod farms. Seed is scarce because it is slow to germinate. Regular mowing is essential, because this stiff grass proves difficult to cut if left too long. It is very cold tolerant, but most varieties go dormant early and green up late in spring, so it is not a popular choice in the North.

bermudagrass (*Cynodon* spp.)

Common Bermudagrass (*Cynodon dactylon*) is a warm-season, medium-texture grass that performs best in sunny areas, is heat and drought tolerant, and is insect and disease resistant. It grows easily from seed in poor soils, so it's tempting to use to create an attractive, large lawn in a short time for little cost. The primary chore with this turf is edging. Bermudagrass spreads by sending out stolons that rival kudzu for speed and tenacity. It often causes problems when it jumps edging and roots in flower beds. Selective herbicides may kill Bermudagrasses, leaving most other plants unharmed. Improved hybrids are finer, denser, and lower growing than common Bermudagrass. They still spread rapidly, but because they don't produce viable seed, they are better-behaved. Bermudagrass does not tolerate cold winters, but it is a popular choice for warm regions of the United States.

ryegrass (*Lolium* spp.)

Two main types of ryegrass exist—annual ryegrass (*Lolium multiflorum*) and perennial ryegrass (*L. perenne*). Both are cool-season grasses that germinate quickly from seed. As the name implies, annual ryegrass lives for only a year. It is often used to cover bare soil until a permanent grass fills in, but it is aggressive and may crowd out perennial grasses you grow with it. Perennial ryegrass is a tough, fine-textured bunchgrass that withstands traffic and can serve as a nurse grass or to overseed warm-season turf for a green winter lawn. Even with a sharp mower blade, this wiry grass tends to create split ends, giving the lawn a white cast. Perennial ryegrass is often mixed with Kentucky bluegrass to form wear-resistant turf for sports fields and playgrounds. It may struggle in severely cold winters, but bluegrass should fill in.

kentucky bluegrass (*Poa pratensis*)

When you hear those exquisite fine-textured, lawns calling out to you from the pictures on the fertilizer bags at the garden center, chances are you're hearing the call of Kentucky bluegrass. Easily established by seed or sod, it spreads quickly by underground rhizomes to form a high-quality lawn. This cool-season grass has shallow roots, so it requires regular irrigation. Drought conditions force it into dormancy, but it quickly recovers when water becomes available again. It does best in the northern United States, where short summers and ample rainfall allow it to live up to its potential. It does not tolerate excessive wear and tear. If you have kids or dogs or like to play sports, look for a blend with named cultivars of Kentucky bluegrass.

▲ Layers of plants from floor to ceiling and a simple patio transformed this abandoned city lot into an urban Eden.

A A carpet of fescue
C 'Tifway' Bermudagrass
B 'Emerald' zoysiagrass
D 'Penn-Fine' perennial ryegrass

behind garden walls

Walls are valuable tools. They shelter garden rooms from buffeting winds, provide warmth for people and plants, screen unsightly views, divide properties, lend structure to the garden, and retain soil. They also provide security. A high fence or masonry wall keeps children and pets contained and helps protect against trespassers. The most popular reason for a wall, however, is privacy.

From a design perspective, walls help narrow the visual field and direct your attention toward a particular feature. This creates a more intriguing design and aids circulation. By screening out all views except a line of sight toward a garden bench or other attraction, you effectively guide people to that spot. Continue this trick throughout your garden to lure people in the direction you want them to stroll. Improve the effect by always giving a hint of another view around the bend.

Garden walls can be fashioned from stone, brick, concrete, stucco, wood, metal, or a thick hedge. When selecting a material for your wall, keep your house and other buildings in mind. Plants can blend in with any scheme, but masonry should harmonize with the materials used on the home. This doesn't mean a brick home must have a brick wall—too much of one material can be overwhelming. Consider a stucco wall with brick coping as a way to complement a brick home.

The high cost of masonry has inspired modern manufacturers to invent various systems of interlocking concrete-block retaining walls that bend the land to our will. Attractive models are not exactly cheap, but they are easier to erect than brick walls, so you save on labor expenses. They aren't right for every residential situation, but their popularity has inspired attractive products that include distressed blocks available in several shapes that fit together to give a wall the random appearance of an old stone wall. Some blocks have hollow planting pockets you can fill with soil and trailing plants to create a living wall.

Hedges are a popular method for forming garden walls. Their main drawback is the time it takes to form a thick barrier. Arborvitaes (*Thuja* spp.) and Leyland cypress (×*Cupressocyparis leylandii*) are valued for their naturally tidy shape, which requires little pruning. If you want a geometric hedge with sharp edges, some maintenance will always be involved, but if you find pleasure in the whir of the lawn mower as it leaves behind tidy rows of turf, you will likely enjoy mastering a pair of hedge shears. The manual type is much quieter and preferred for small hedges. Electric or gas-powered shears are noisier and higher maintenance, but they can save much time and effort on large hedges. (For more on hedges, see pages 140–141.)

◄ Garden walls don't need to be solid to create effective private havens.

◄ A wall of evergreens creates privacy and acts as a foil for a colorful border.

◄ A tall hedge of Leyland cypress creates a fast-growing screen between neighboring properties.

▶ Masonry walls are relatively expensive, but they offer low upkeep and timeless beauty.

▶▶ This arborvitae hedge muffles road noise and adds a third dimension to an otherwise flat garden.

give me shelter

The only ceiling many people want in their garden is the sky overhead. Confined by the ceilings inside their homes, businesses, and even their vehicles when they're between the two places, the garden is the place to enjoy the great outdoors. Why would you want a ceiling there?

Outdoor ceilings serve several functions. They shelter us from sun and wind, give us privacy, and provide the third dimension of depth to the length and width of a garden. They also provide a sense of enclosure and security. As with walls, an outdoor ceiling can consist of living plants or constructed materials or a combination of the two.

Anyone who grew up in the United States before 1960 can probably recall the arching cathedral ceilings created by the American elms that once lined streets throughout the country. Unfortunately Dutch elm disease devastated many of these grand trees. If you want this type of ceiling, improved varieties of elms and plenty of other trees will form a towering canopy over your landscape. Depending on the area of the country you live in, you might select a canopy of oaks, maples, poplars, white pines, hemlocks, redwoods, or other trees that reach 75 feet or more. Be sure you have ample room for a large tree without having to prune it and risk ruining its natural form. And remember that you (and your lawn) will have to adapt by expanding mulched areas or groundcovers around the tree, overseeding with shade-tolerant varieties of grass, or completely replacing your sun-worshiping turf.

A faster way to achieve an outdoor ceiling is to construct an arbor, pergola, gazebo, or other overhead structure. A pergola is essentially a linear arbor often used to shade pathways. It originated in Italy, where it provided shade and a support for grapevines. If you're looking for flowers and fragrance to cover your pergola, choices include jasmine, jessamine, wisteria, roses, akebia, and autumn clematis. Make sure your building material is well-preserved if you plan to grow plants on it; vines trap moisture against the surface and encourage rot and rust. Rather than attaching posts or lattice directly to a fence or wall, leave a gap of at least several inches to allow access for maintenance work. If you want your structure to last, twining vines need to be cut back severely every few years to apply an annual coat of stain or wood preservative. Stains are easier to maintain than paint because they don't peel and require no scraping. Metal requires less maintenance, but it's a bigger expense up front. Nothing quite matches the elegance of old wrought iron, although some attractive aluminum structures come close, and they last just as long or longer.

When connected to the home, these ceiling structures make for a smooth transition between indoors and out, especially when furnished with tables, chairs, lounges, and other comforts of home. Arbors, gazebos, and other shelters sited in the far reaches of a garden will entice visitors to explore. Butted up against a fence or wall, they provide an added measure of privacy. An overhead structure will shroud you from neighboring upper-story windows, a service the average fence, wall, or hedge cannot provide.

🔖🔖 A high canopy of tulip poplars and an understory of flowering dogwoods provide a majestic ceiling for this naturalistic garden.

🔖 A formal arbor sets the stage for the elegant rose garden to come.

◄ Though it holds little value in terms of true shelter, this rustic structure invites visitors to sit a spell and enjoy the view.

▲ A series of rustic arches festooned with grapevines serve as walls and ceiling, directing visitors to the wooden bench.

playing with a full deck

Decks play important roles in many lawnscapes, not the least of which is to provide a smooth transition between the house and the lawn. They should be versatile enough to improve your outdoor living and be integrated with your home, yard, garden, and pathways.

Most new-home decks are too small to meet the needs of the family. When designing a deck, think of it as more than a spot to set up a table and four chairs. Look for ways to provide lots of options—a covered, screened area for bug-free dining and rainy days; a sunny area for soaking up rays on a cool day; an open area to gather with friends; a quiet niche for reading ; and storage space.

Railings are essential on most decks. Specifications are determined by local building codes, and typically you'll need a railing for any deck that stands 18 inches or more above ground level. Codes also specify distances between posts, the gap under the railing, and rail spacing, which typically is no more than 6 inches. Creative options for railings are many, including plexiglass, stainless-steel cables, copper pipe, and twig fencing. Select material that matches your home architecture and your deck style.

Remember the extras when planning a deck. Built-in benches can double as railings and even do triple duty as dry storage for seat cushions, candles, coolers, umbrellas, and other handy items. Outdoor kitchens complete with grill, refrigerator, sink, and trash cans will help you get more use out your deck. Built-in planters are a great way to add color and life to a deck, and they're particularly handy for growing herbs for indoor and outdoor cooking. A small potting bench is a convenient accessory if you plan to have a container garden on the deck.

Outdoor spas are popular deck add-ons. They are best installed with a new deck, but you can retrofit them. Their added weight requires reinforced joists and beams, and it's easier to install the plumbing and electricity before decking goes down. You'll also want an access panel to reach the filter and heater for maintenance. Consider a trellis or arbor for privacy.

Don't overlook landscape lighting options to extend the hours spent on your deck and to make it safer. Professionally installed line-voltage systems are costly, although you get the added convenience of outlets, ceiling fans, and floodlights. Less expensive low-voltage systems are homeowner-friendly and are much more attractive than the black plastic runway lights typical of the older style of landscape lighting.

Second-story decks allow you to survey your domain.

This cedar deck connects the indoor family room to the lawn. A slight elevation change allowed the builder to dispense with handrails.

A series of decks, steps, and landings ease the transition from the house to the lawn.

on the cutting edge

Traditionally you had three choices in decking material: treated pine, cedar, or redwood. Technology and environmental concerns have inspired a host of options. Here is a summary of what's available:

Aluminum—This sturdy, lightweight, long-lasting material should be coated with a textured finish to keep it cooler in the sun and provide traction when wet. Fire, insects, and decay are not an issue. Some manufacturers make watertight aluminum decking that keeps the area below dry. Requires professional installation.

Brazilian walnut—This hardwood comes from ipe trees (*Tabebuia* spp.) harvested from managed tropical forests. It's twice as heavy and costs two to three times more than pine, but it lasts five times longer. Even without preservative, ipe is resistant to termites and water rot, and it has the same fire rating as concrete and steel. It requires predrilled holes and screws.

Composite—This environmentally responsible material made from recovered wood fiber and recycled plastic can be cut, drilled, and sanded like conventional lumber. When allowed to weather for several months, the wood fiber helps it hold a stain. It is highly resistant to insects and rot. Hollow posts and rails are great for running wiring for lighting.

Rubber—Commonly known in the trade as Rumber, this material is composed of recycled tires and plastic. It is virtually impermeable to water, UV rays, and insects, making it great for docks and other wet environments. Limited colors include light gray, dark gray, and terracotta. It puts a nice spring in your step. It is not suited for substructure use.

Treated pine—Treated pine isn't new, but the way it's being treated is. Most new products contain a copper-based preservative or sodium dimethyldithio-carbamate (DDC) rather than arsenate. Some manufacturers offer a lifetime guarantee against insects and decay.

Vinyl—Vinyl decking is available in custom colors. The color is solid, so scratches don't show. It's weather and fire resistant. UV inhibitors help preserve color, prevent cracking and warping, and make it cool under bare feet even in full sun. It can't be used for substructures and requires professional installation.

▸ A satellite patio provides a secluded escape and allows you to utilize space at the back of your property.

▾ Turf and flagstone provide a natural shift from the lawn to the home's interior.

⤙ A well-placed patio provides a clean, dry surface for coming and going, reducing the amount of mud, grass clippings, and other debris tracked inside.

on solid ground

When a deck is the only outdoor room in a landscape, people often long for solid ground beneath their feet. Patios and terraces provide a connection to the rest of the yard. Even if you already have a deck, consider adding a patio at the base of the steps to improve the passage into the garden. A well-used deck often leads to substantial foot traffic that kills the grass at the bottom of the steps. A narrow path leading from the steps won't provide the choice of directions a patio does. A patio in this location serves as an oversize landing and is a pleasant contrast to the grass and plants in the yard.

Installing a patio is a project well within the abilities of most homeowners, particularly a gravel or dry-set patio. It takes time, money, and an eye for detail, and it's a project that repays with low upkeep and years of enjoyment.

To look its best and function properly, a patio must be installed properly and have good drainage. Various surfaces drain at different rates. Water on a smooth slate patio set in mortar will run off faster than on a patio of loose gravel, so the gravel surface will need more slope to ensure good drainage. A patio made of gravel or dry-laid bricks or stone (no mortar) slows the runoff, allowing water to seep into the ground. In regions of the country where underground aquifers are running dry, builders and homeowners are encouraged (sometimes required) to minimize paved surfaces. No matter what material you choose, you may need to install drains or other erosion-control methods on or around a patio. If you must locate a patio in an area that receives a lot of rainfall, be sure to install some type of drainage system. (See page 116).

When it comes to selecting material for your patio, you have several choices. There is a fundamental satisfaction in using indigenous materials, and you can temper the cost by mixing in less expensive concrete pavers. Concrete is not the dull, flat gray stuff it used to be. With various aggregates, mix-in dyes, stamped patterns, mosaic tiles, and textures added with brushes, leaves, boards, rock salt, and other elements, you can create a patio that has personality. You can even mix two or more materials to create interest. It takes skill to work with materials that vary in size. Although different thicknesses are particularly tricky, a 2-inch sand-setting bed allows you to adjust up or down. No matter how careful you are, some settling will always occur after completion, so hold back a little sand and use it for fine-tuning future dips and irregularities.

step-by-step patio

step 1. Whatever surface you choose, it's critical to get the base right. The most labor-intensive job is excavating. Dig down 6 inches plus the depth of your paver without disturbing the subsoil. For large patios, rent a skid steer. For smaller patios, a wheelbarrow, shovel, and muscle power will work. Transfer topsoil to the garden. If you hit clay or rock, seek a neighbor or construction site that needs fill dirt.

step 2. Fill with 4 inches of finely crushed gravel (also called stone dust or crusher run) and tamp it. You can rent a power tamper to cover a large area quickly, but a manual tamper is less expensive and will be available as you complete your project over time.

step 3. A layer of landscape fabric on top of the gravel will limit weeds, but it's not essential. Most weeds can sprout in the sand between the pavers.

step 4. Add 2 inches of construction sand, level it, wet it with a fine spray from the hose, and tamp it.

step 5. Now you're ready to lay your surface. Safety goggles, a carpenter's level, a rubber mallet, a mason's chisel, and a hand sledge are essential tools. For accurate cuts, use an electric circular saw with a masonry blade.

◀ The inspiration for this barefoot-cool decking of Arizona flagstone and turf came from singer Jimmy Buffet's pool, which was featured in a magazine.

▼ A livable landscape is all about providing options for gathering places.

a room with a view

A terrace is a close relative of the patio and the deck. To qualify as a terrace, an area should adjoin the home on one side and be raised to offer a view. It can be thought of as a patio that functions as a raised deck.

Farmers in China and Egypt have been leveling terraces to cultivate crops on steep slopes for centuries. In Italy during the Renaissance, these hillside gardens were modified to become outdoor

rooms designed for leisure more than farming. Extending from the downhill sides of villas, terraces provided a natural solution to the need for social gathering spots on hilly Italian terrain. By the 17th century, terraces were commonplace on European mansions. The terrace provided a valuable service earlier protected courtyards could not—a grand stage where gatherers could lounge and stroll, surveying the formal gardens and workers below.

Modern terraces tend to be more modest than their well-to-do forebears. Instead of grand overlooks composed of marble tiles and balustrades, they are more likely located on a roof above a garage with a ceramic tile or brick floor and iron railings. If your home is situated on a slope, consider a terrace to create living space on the downhill side. By cutting into the uphill side of the slope and filling on the downhill side, you can create a level platform. Make sure it drains slightly away from the house. You may need a retaining wall to hold back the loose fill dirt. Generally, if the wall is higher than 2 feet and located less than 6 feet from the house, it will require the approval of a building inspector.

A terrace doesn't require a large area. A narrow strip running the length of the house can provide room for the family to gather and improve the flow of foot traffic. Whether located in the front of the home or the back, a terrace is an elegant addition that will provide a firm connection to the earth and perhaps a place to stroll as you take in the breeze and survey your kingdom, even if it's only your tomato plants growing 6 inches below.

material world

Here are a few of the common choices for a dry-set patio or terrace.

bricks are available in virtually every earth-tone color. The nominal size is 8×4 inches, but the actual size is 7⅝×3⅝ to allow room for mortar joints. Use SW-(severe weather) grade bricks for patios.

granite is popular in the northeast, where it is plentiful. It is hard and durable and has a beautiful, speckled pattern. Colors include charcoal gray, carnelian, and salt-and-pepper.

limestone (photo A) is soft enough to make it easy to work with but durable enough to make a long-lasting patio. Select dressed limestone, which has been cut on all sides, for a smooth patio.

patio blocks come in a range of sizes, typically 24×24, 12×12, or 12×6 inches. When set on a bed of sand, these concrete slabs are the fastest way to lay down a patio. They are available in a variety of colors with stamped patterns and exposed aggregate surfaces.

pavers (photo B) made of earth-tone concrete are more durable than clay bricks. Rated as SX for severe weather or MS for moderate weather, they are graded according to the load they can bear. Buy the highest grade for a driveway or parking pad. Pavers come in a true 8×4-inch size, as well as hexagons, key shapes, and square cobblestones.

sandstone (photo C) is a porous natural stone in colors streaked with tan, yellow, brown, orange, and red. It is sometimes referred to as fieldstone because it is usually dug from fields, not quarried.

slate is a fine-grain, natural stone that can be split cleanly into thin pieces. Quality varies greatly, so select slate that does not crumble. It is available in blue, gray, deep purple, and charcoal.

◄ Patios removed from the bustle of the house are like open-air parlors. Be sure to equip yours with furniture that invites people to interact.

satellite decks and patios

Patios, decks, and terraces near the home bring nature to you, but a satellite deck or patio set away from the house is a way to bring you to nature. Satellite spaces are ideal for establishing a quiet retreat. A peaceful nook where family members can escape for quiet contemplation or an intimate conversation can be as valuable as a larger outdoor gathering place meant for dining and entertaining. Satellite spaces can also be a strong draw during social gatherings when a couple or two need a break from the action.

To help draw visitors out to a satellite garden room, offer a few hints that great things await those who go exploring. A path leading the way can be a subtle or an obvious clue. Other clues include a gazebo, arbor, canopy, or other structure peeking from behind the sheltering foliage. A pond or fountain offering the sound of splashing water and the warmth of a fire pit are both strong lures. A special objet d'art, such as a glimmering gazing ball, will grab someone's eye and lead the viewer down a path of discovery.

Use a satellite area to increase the usable space in your landscape. If most of your garden is cool and shady, build a deck in a sunny clearing. If your garden is open to full, blistering sun and the prying eyes of neighbors and passersby, tuck a patio into a secluded, shady corner. If no shady corner exists, create shade with a gazebo, canopy, or vine-covered structure. If your only outdoor space is a raised deck, create a small terrace where you can set your feet on solid ground. It all goes back to that critical site analysis. Figure out where you could most benefit from a satellite garden room and then think about the style and materials that will best achieve your goal.

◥ A spa or other feature accompanying your remote garden room will ensure it gets plenty of use.

◥ A satellite patio need not be located in the back forty to be effective. This one is just a few steps from the main patio.

▶ A grassy carpet leads the way to a gazebo. As the name implies, a gazebo's essential qualification is that it provides whoever is inside a scene to gaze upon.

▶▶ Always take into consideration how you will access your satellite gathering spot. This design provides a slow route (curved steps) and a fast route (water slide).

make room for kids

Gardening may not have the glitz and bleeps of the high-tech world, but the great outdoors does hold a strange fascination for kids. If you want to give computer games and 24-hour cartoon cable networks a run for their money, there are several ways to get your kids into the garden.

When it comes to lawns, most young children just want the pleasure of a soft, green playground where they can tumble, picnic, and roll their balls and trucks. Some kids relish playing the part of a superhero who can crush grubs with a single stomp or yank evil knotweed from the lawn. On a warm summer day, most kids are willing to help set up the lawn sprinkler and move it around the yard, although mowing should be left to adults. However, you may see a major interest surge in lawn care during the teen years, when kids learn there is money to be made each week by taking on the job of mowing.

A better way to interest children in the garden is to give them their own space with their own plants to tend. Edible plants are always popular with kids, but a lesson on what plants are OK to taste is a must. Mark plants with fun labels that designate them as safe for tasting. Planting seeds is probably the most exciting part of gardening. Kids are usually willing to help water every few days, although they might "accidentally" get as much water on themselves as they do on the plants. Older children can be taught how to feed hungry plants with a water-soluble fertilizer every few weeks. Harvesting is also a favorite chore. Children with a higher level of interest can learn how to thin young seedlings, pinch herbs, deadhead spent blooms, and snip flowers to help spur more growth.

Kids have the attention spans of butterflies and hummingbirds, which may be why they are interested in plants that attract these winged jewels. Plant red salvia, petunias, hibiscus, monkey flower, cross vine, and trumpet creeper to draw hummingbirds, and butterfly bush, butterfly weed, coneflowers, zinnias, lantana, and pentas to attract butterflies. Setting out a few extra plants to allow for losses to pests teaches kids about integrated pest management. You can also order beneficial ladybugs, green lacewings, and praying mantis egg casings to release into the garden with an explanation of the laws of the jungle.

Many companies have picked up on children's love of gardening and now make kid-size wheelbarrows, trowels, watering cans, rakes, and a host of other tools. Fun aprons, gloves, hats, rubber boots, and other garden gear make for easy cleanup. Having their own tools and gardening garb makes it fun and allows kids to immerse themselves in their work. It's also less stressful for Mom and Dad, who don't have to worry about their good tools being lost or broken or getting mud and grass stains out of their child's Sunday best. Remember to have fun garden projects on hand for a rainy day, such as building birdhouses, seed-starting kits, and creating mosaic pottery. The finished results can be moved into the garden.

◄◄Gardens that accommodate kids can be artful, colorful, and inviting.

◄ This compact playground was designed to be adaptable. When the kids are grown, the equipment will be removed and the mulched area beneath the tree planted with a shade-tolerant groundcover.

◄ This urban oasis provides a safe haven for kids. With any kid space, consider adding a nearby patio, deck, or other gathering spot where adults can enjoy their own activities and be close at hand.

plants with kid appeal

Plants that hold magic for kids generally have large seeds, sprout and grow quickly, produce fruit, have a touchable quality, or have an interesting name, fragrance, appearance, or taste. Here are some suggestions to help get your child growing:

Beans

Blueberries

Butterfly weed

Carrots ('Little Finger')

Chinese lantern

Chives

Corn ('Mini-Blue')

Dill

Eggplant ('Ghostbuster')

Elephant's ears

Gourds ('Speckled Swan')

Lamb's-ears

Lemon balm

Mint

Money plant

Moonflower

Morning glory

Nasturtium

Parsley

Peas

Pumpkins ('Cinderella', 'Wee-B-Little', and 'Baby Boo')

Radishes

Rosemary

Snapdragons

Strawberries

Sunflowers ('Paul Bunyan', 'Giganteus', and 'The Joker')

Tomatoes ('Tiny Tim')

Watermelon ('Moon and Stars' and 'Sugar Baby')

Zinnias ('Peter Pan', 'Small World', and 'Whirligig')

Zucchini

lawn play

Whether it's a neighborhood volleyball match or a game of lawn chess for two, more families are rediscovering that the backyard is a great place to gather for lawn games and sports. By providing a place at home where kids and adults can play, you make your landscape more usable. This use can range from getting in some quality practice time whenever you have a few spare moments to entertaining during cookouts.

Most lawn games simply require a flat area of grass free of trees, poles, and other obstacles. Golf, soccer, football, kick ball, bocce, croquet, cricket, volleyball, badminton, and horseshoes can all be played on a modest plot of lawn, although it may require some modification of the standard playing field and a little latitude with the rules. The more versatile your landscape is, the more your entire family will use it.

Next to a herd of hungry deer or a family of armadillos, the lawn fanatic's worst nightmare is a teenager armed with cleats and a soccer ball practicing a bicycle kick or the family golfer hacking away with a 9-iron on the front lawn. Find ways to make everyone happy. If you have a sloping lot, consider terracing it to create several levels. Use the lowest level for lawn sports so that no one takes a tumble diving for a ball or shuttlecock. The second level could be a deck, patio, or gazebo that can serve as bleachers. Another level could be a vegetable garden, a perennial cutting garden, or a private retreat. It's nice to have this area so that people can seek solitude and delicate plants can remain a safe distance from balls and players gone astray from the game area. The same design principle can be used with a level yard. Just lay out several garden rooms instead of terraces. Use sturdy fencing, berms, or tough hedges to separate the play lawn from the dainty plants, fragile garden art, and delicate structures.

For homeowners who want to guarantee the preservation of their lawn, companies design and install residential sport courts with surfaces made from a concrete pad covered with acrylic, polypropylene, or rubber. Most are typically half the size of a tennis court. High fencing can be painted black and outfitted with ornamental aluminum gates to keep balls and kids within bounds. Surround the fencing with thick, dark green foliage to help it blend with the surrounding landscape. These multipurpose game courts don't accommodate golf or football as well as a lawn does, but they are ideal for basketball, handball, paddle tennis, skateboarding, and roller hockey. Kids can even ride their bikes on larger courts.

⬋ A safe, fair playing field requires a flat lawn free of overhead obstructions such as tree branches and utility lines.

⬈ Penalty kicks are no problem when the lawn is surrounded by stiff hedges and tough natural plantings.

⬉ Croquet is a favorite lawn sport.

◂ Few lawn sports are easier to learn or less expensive to play than badminton.

◀ If you intend to play lawn games such as boccie-ball or croquet, consider a border of tough wildflowers, a garden wall, or both.

putting on the green

Professional or amateur, any golfer will tell you that mastering the short game is the best way to keep your score down. With the right kind of lawn, you can practice chipping and putting and never leave the comfort of your own yard. Companies specialize in designing gardens that double as small golf courses, or you can design your own.

Begin with a small, smooth, putting-green lawn surrounded by an apron of tall fescue, Kentucky bluegrass, or Bermudagrass, depending on location. Bentgrass is ideal for greens, although it requires special care, including a mower that can be lowered to less than an inch. (Some pro courses maintain their bentgrass at $1/10$ of an inch.)

Bentgrass also grows by wiry stolons and shallow roots that require frequent fertilization and lots of water, which in turn lead to a thick layer of thatch. Frequent aeration and dethatching are needed to get water and nutrients to the roots. In addition you'll need to control the wide variety of fungal diseases. In short, it's not a turf for anyone seeking a low-maintenance lawn. However, if your mind is made up and nothing else will suffice for your backyard green, select 'Astoria' or 'Exeter', both of which are manageable in small doses. In some areas, hybrid Bermudagrasses are an acceptable substitute in warm climates. They can be mown down to $1/4$ inch and are less needy than bentgrass.

To finish your course and your landscape, find ways to integrate attractive and functional features. Install sand bunkers that double as sandboxes for kids. Water hazards can also be fountains, and the roughs can be mulched beds filled with low-growing ornamental grasses or other groundcovers. If you plan carefully, you should still have room around the perimeter to nestle in patios, decks, cooking areas, and other elements to attract nongolfers.

▶ Grass is a given for lawn sports. What other surface can repair itself with a little sunshine, water, fertilizer, and aeration?

be a good sport

Here are some tips to help you create your own sports complex:

- Integrate play areas with standard landscape features. Sand traps and horseshoe pits can also be used to build sand castles. A water hazard can serve as a koi pond. Reserve a few bins in the toolshed for sporting equipment. A patio of alternating light and dark pavers can be used for a grand checkerboard or chessboard.

- A formal rectangular lawn edged with stone can function as a standard court for lawn sports such as bocce or croquet. Edging helps prevent balls from rolling into the street or surrounding flower beds.

- Good drainage is important for all lawns but particularly critical for a lawn used for games. Although a slight slope to one side will work fine, a lawn that is slightly higher in the center and pitches toward the edges makes for a better play surface.

- Select hardy plants that can survive a little trampling, especially if you are a golfer who subscribes to the "play it where it lies" rule. Cotoneaster, heather, lamb's-ears, ornamental blue fescue, euonymus, ajuga, creeping thyme, and vinca are a few low-growing options.

- Avoid prickly plants such as roses, Chinese hollies, and barberries.

- To make a trampoline safer for the jumpers and less obtrusive, select a clear area of the yard, dig a pit with a drain, and place the trampoline over the pit.

- Grasses with the best wear resistance are perennial ryegrass/Kentucky bluegrass blends, tall fescue, Bermudagrass, and buffalograss.

⏶ With four boys, the homeowners decided this paved games court was the best option for their high-traffic backyard. The sandpits on both ends of the horseshoe court double as sandboxes.

▲ Lawn games such as cricket mean fun times, family interaction, and good old-fashioned exercise.

completing the picture

Patios, decks, sport courts, and other garden rooms are natural places to start when designing a landscape. However, just as life is made up of more than holidays and birthdays, landscapes must include more than special attractions. They also need transition zones, pathways and steps, and functional service areas that play second fiddle to the headliners. It's easy to overlook these features or squeeze them in after the fact, but giving them the necessary attention in the design stage can mean the difference between a good landscape and a less-than-satisfactory one. Presenting a total package requires attention to detail.

▶ To make this tiny courtyard seem larger, it was designed as a series of three rooms. Visitors are drawn from the slate patio near the home to the lawn and then the slate patio at the far end.

blending indoors and out

Every home should have areas that stretch the limits of outdoor living. In the right outdoor setting, the simple acts of sleeping, cooking, eating, and talking become sleeping on a screened porch with serenading crickets and frogs, grilling kabobs over an open flame, dining under starlit skies, and enjoying conversation with friends on the patio. Even mundane activities, such as showering and checking e-mail, become enchanting experiences when done alfresco. While no outdoor room can provide the comforts of home all day long, 365 days per year, when thoughtfully planned and well equipped, outdoor spaces can fulfill many of the functions usually relegated to the indoors.

Archaeologists have shown that the materials used on garden walls and exterior paving in many ancient Roman gardens were just as lavish as those used inside the homes. Skillfully crafted marble slabs, tile mosaics, murals, and stucco reliefs all combined to form true outdoor rooms. The areas blended so well that archaeologists today face the problem of determining where the inside ended and the outside began. Wouldn't it be great if archaeologists 2,000 years from now said the same thing about your home and garden?

The ideal landscape includes natural transitions from indoor living spaces to outdoor ones. The outdoor entry garden should lead to your front door; the patio should be attached to your living or dining area. Make certain the materials used for construction of your outdoor landscape features are compatible with those used indoors. Complementary colors, textures, and furnishings will help blur the lines between indoor and outdoor living.

◄ French doors that
open onto an arbor-
covered patio make this
dining area an extension
of the home.

☛ The soothing sound of
a waterfall draws
visitors outdoors.

▼ A structure doesn't
need four solid walls,
a roof, and a gate to
qualify as a garden
room. Trellises,
columns, fences,
seating walls, plants,
and other features can
lend privacy without
cutting off the rest of
the world.

entryways

When first-time guests arrive at your home, they should have no doubt about where you want them to go. A good design will help them figure out which areas are meant for public access and which ones are private family areas. A heavy, decorative iron gate might mark the entrance to a formal front courtyard, whereas a simple lattice arch festooned with trumpet honeysuckle might be better suited to welcome backyard guests. Your entryway gives visitors their first and last impressions, so it should offer something memorable. You can get away with a few weeds farther down the path, but the entrance should be dazzling. It should act as a gracious host that welcomes visitors to your home or garden and bids them a fond farewell as they depart.

A well-designed entrance helps orient people and make a statement about the experience to come. Select plants and materials appropriate to the area around the entryway. Public entrances call for a fancier gate or arbor, an unusual specimen plant, such as a Japanese maple (*Acer palmatum*), star magnolia (*Magnolia stellata*), or tree peony (*Paeonia* spp.), and nice paving materials, such as cut stone or brick. To mark the entrance to a secret garden, use low-key materials, such as a homemade bent-willow arbor, plants that blend with the rest of the garden, and turf, mulch, or natural stone paving.

Arbors are often used to mark an entryway or to control circulation to and from places around the landscape. Position an entry arbor so that it frames a scene and tells people where they can go. Trim it with materials and colors that match the home. It needs to stand out enough that visitors can locate it easily, yet it should blend with the surrounding garden. If an arbor is going to stand alone, it should look sturdy and have plants anchoring its base. A lone, wispy lattice arbor stuck in the lawn can perform all the technical duties an arbor should—frame a view, mark an entrance or a transition to another area, and create a vertical element in the landscape—and still look out of balance.

Because entryways occur at the threshold of a transition area, they have to match the style of their immediate surroundings as well as the area you're entering. When designing an entryway, think of it from all angles. Although the main focus might be to welcome arriving guests, remember to make it a pleasant experience for your guests as they leave.

➤ Show visitors the door—in a good way. This arbor mimics the home's gables and frames the front door.

➤ Every entry has a unique personality, providing clues about the space inside.

◀◀ For an entry with grace and dignity, this arbor echoes the arch over the front door. As an added invitation, evergreen clematis displays sweet-scented blooms in early spring.

◀ As viewed from the entry, the retaining wall, steps, arbor, and flat lawn present visitors with a green welcome mat.

appealing entries

One way to make an entrance memorable is to make sure it appeals to the five senses—sight, touch, smell, taste, and sound. The same can be said of the entire garden, although an entrance is a good place to intensify the experience.

Plants with eye-catching color or texture are good choices. A few evergreens will form a tapestry of texture that anchors the entrance through all four seasons. Although needle producers such as pines, spruces, and firs are probably the first trees to come to mind, also consider broadleaf evergreen trees and shrubs such as magnolias, rhododendrons, viburnums, hollies, and Indian hawthorn (*Rhaphiolepis indica*). If your front entrance will welcome guests year-round, mix in a few early-spring plants, such as Lenten rose (*Helleborus orientalis*), spring bulbs, or wintersweet (*Chimonanthus praecox*) and some plants with late-season interest, such as chrysanthemums and ornamental grasses.

Although all plants have texture, think of some that offer extremes. Soft lamb's-ears (*Stachys byzantina*), wormwood (*Artemisia* spp.), rose campion (*Lychnis coronaria*), and sage (*Salvia* spp.) beg to be touched by every passerby. Cactus, yuccas, roses, and other prickly plants are OK planted a safe distance from the path. You also can get the same spiky texture from iris, crocosmia, lavender, and many softer ornamental grasses.

➤ In this Oregon garden, the threshold between cultivated garden and woodlands is clearly defined by a torii, a Japanese structure traditionally used as a gateway to a Shinto shrine.

◂ The entrance to this backyard cottage garden well-stocked with old-fashioned peonies, irises, geraniums, and roses is appropriately informal.

Plant fragrant flowering vines that will cast their magic spell on people walking through an entry arbor. If you have enough space and a strong supporting structure, mix several vines with staggered bloom times to extend the season. Plant musky boxwoods or sharp-smelling herbs such as anise, mint, germander, or rosemary where passersby will brush against them and release their pungent fragrance. Creeping thyme and oregano planted in the sunny crevices of paths will release their heady aromas when visitors tread on their foliage.

Remember taste in the entrance garden. Herbs such as parsley, arugula, and dill are nice to nibble in small amounts. Vining and cane fruits such as grapes, cherry tomatoes, thornless raspberries or blackberries, and any other edible fruits that are convenient to pluck and taste as you pass through an arbor will intensify the entry experience.

Take advantage of breezes by hanging tinkling wind chimes and planting ornamental grasses that whisper in the wind. A bubbling fountain will attract songbirds and appeal to the ears, adding subtle charm to the entryway.

getting there from here

Well-placed paths draw you from one place to another, linking you with places you want and need to visit. Wherever you're going, paths should take you there in comfort and style. They can be straight or meandering, narrow or wide, sophisticated or casual.

As with all garden features, the key is to select materials and a design that capture the spirit of the setting. You may want a straight, wide, paved path to usher visitors to an elegant terrace or to greet them at the guest parking area and lead them to the front door. These settings call for marble, brick, tile, limestone, slate, or other cut stone that lends a ceremonial touch. Take clues from the home's building material, perhaps picking up on limestone keystones or a slate porch.

If the purpose of your path is to hold down the mud along the route between the doghouse and the back door or to show the way to a satellite gazebo, you won't need anything quite so formal and costly. These secluded paths are often the most fun to create and traverse. Hidden from public view, you are free to use your ingenuity and imagination to explore alternative materials. In a woodland setting, you can use wood chips, which often come free from local tree-trimming companies. Other mulches such as bark, pine straw, or chopped leaves also lend a natural touch. To emphasize the connection with nature, inset wood rounds into the organic mulch to serve as stepping-stones.

If you want something other than mulch, use loose stone such as decomposed granite, crushed

brick, crusher run, or pea gravel. When using pea gravel, first lay down a base of crusher run or other material that will pack firmly, then top it off with 2 inches of pea gravel. Pea gravel and other river-washed stones that don't compact are difficult to walk through and can bog down a wheelbarrow if they are more than 2 inches deep.

Edging is important for keeping gravel and mulch contained on pathways. Consider recycled materials such as overturned glass bottles (champagne bottles are sturdiest), terra-cotta roof tiles, or cedar logs (laid horizontally or stood on end). Although it lasts only a season or two, wattle edging formed from woven branches trimmed from the garden is another economical way to lend charming cottage-garden style to a path.

Concrete offers durability, economy, and great flexibility. Precast concrete brick pavers, stepping-stones, and patio pavers are available in hundreds of colors and shapes that can inspire an infinite range of path styles. Poured concrete walkways don't have to be as homely and lifeless as a city sidewalk. If you already have a concrete surface, you can alter it with stains to give it a contemporary design or a faux antique patina. For freshly poured concrete, you can achieve a variety of styles by applying powdered dyes, scoring, stamping, or imprinting or embedding tiles, pebbles, marbles, and other personal touches before it hardens. Precise forms used by contractors to create perfect edges aren't always necessary. If you mix the concrete on the stiff side, you can use a loose, troweled edge for a free-form path that's appropriate for a casual setting. You can also try your hand at creating individual faux stones for an informal path. Distress them by using a sponge to dab on muddled paint and faux lichen. Start small and in an inconspicuous location until you perfect your technique.

◄◄◄ A first-rate greenhouse or toolshed such as this deserves better than a beeline path of utilitarian concete. Turf lends a softer, more attractive tread for the pathway.

◄◄ Paths provide choices. Proving that lawns don't have to be rigid rectangular plots, this lawn plays a supporting role to billowing beds of sedum, yucca, red hot poker, butterfly bush, and crocosmia.

◄ Overturned wine bottles are an effective, attractive edging. In the "shabby chic" landscape school, they are known as the poor man's stained glass.

the path
less traveled

Of all the options for creating a path, turf is arguably the most lush and inviting. Although not usually the best option for getting you from the driveway to the door of your house, turf is a viable alternative for less-traveled paths. It is soft, tough, and alive. Whereas hardscape paths tend to relate more to the architecture and stand apart from plantings, the rich green color and fine texture of grass act as a subtle foil for surrounding plants. A mown path through a wildflower meadow provides access to nature and makes it a treasured experience. It also lets neighbors know this is an intentional part of the garden, not just a weedy field. In the urban garden, a grassy path softens the harsh surroundings of brick and concrete.

During the design phase of your landscaping, plan your grassy path in a low-traffic, sunny area. Shady sites spell trouble for a grass path. The size and shape of your path should be in scale with surrounding beds. If you want a path to sweep through an area that is bound on both sides by wide perennial beds, make the grass path wide enough to carry some visual weight. Garden designers often design paths to be approximately half the width of the adjacent beds. For a more dynamic landscape, vary the width by rhythmically expanding and pinching in the edges to lend different experiences to the route. A narrow path beside narrow beds with small plantings can give the pedestrian a grand feeling of inflated importance. Follow that experience with a wide path between wide beds to let people appreciate the awesome beauty of nature. For those with a practical side, consider making pathways the same width (or multiples of the width) of your lawn mower and fertilizer spreader.

↗ A ribbon of brick or stone edging wide enough for a wheelbarrow tire will help preserve your turf.

↗ There is no straying from this direct route. The broad path is in proportion to the expansive borders.

◀◀ A woven garden path encourages ambling.

◀ Occasional passes with the lawn mower make this wildflower meadow accessible.

caring for a living path

A successful grass path requires a little extra attention, particularly in the areas of irrigation and aeration.

• Use a garden hose, brightly colored extension cord, or marking paint as a guide for laying out the edge of a new grass path or renovating the edge of an old path that has wandered off course through the years. Make a pass with your mower (while the blade is disengaged) to make sure you can mow it in a single run. Curves that are too sharp add to mowing and trimming time and aren't as easy on the eyes as a gentle curve.

• Deep shade and large, shallow-rooted trees spell trouble for a grass path. Prune off the lower branches to provide more sunlight on your path and irrigate frequently if tree roots are stealing water from the turf.

• Heavy gas-powered aerators are great for covering large lawns, but it's convenient to own a manual one you can take out of your toolshed to breathe a little life into a grassy path.

• Follow the aeration with a topdressing of weed-free compost or sphagnum/compost blend, known as lawn soil, to fill the holes with a light, spongy material that adds nutrients to your lawn, allows roots access to air and water, and further alleviates compaction. Not always practical for an entire lawn, topdressing is a manageable task on grass paths.

• If your cool-season grass path wears thin, use a power rake to scratch the surface of the soil and overseed with a wear-resistant grass variety such as perennial ryegrass or tall fescue in midspring or late summer. For warm-season grasses that are difficult to grow from seed, such as zoysiagrass or hybrid Bermudagrass, use a garden fork to loosen bare patches and plant plugs of sod in midspring.

• If you continue to have problems maintaining a grass path due to foot traffic, add flagstones or stepping-stones to alleviate compaction.

step lively

People naturally gravitate toward a comfortable set of steps. Steps lead you from one elevation in the landscape to another, creating a dynamic flow of traffic and scenery.

Grassy steps are the natural way to extend a grassy path. Maintenance and materials for steps are basically the same as for paths. However, grassy steps are even more susceptible to compaction because the force exerted by ascending and descending people is much greater than when simply strolling along a path. If regular aeration and irrigation fail to keep your steps green and lush, add stepping-stones where the grass is thin on the steps.

Whenever you construct steps of any kind, take care to use a tread surface that provides good traction. Steps in moist, shady areas are particularly prone to forming hazardous moss and mildew, so you may need to powerwash or scrub them periodically. If you think your outdoor steps will serve as an impromptu amphitheater, install a stone or wood edge to provide dry seating when the grass is wet.

Although most people just feel their way through the construction of steps, designing as they build, professional designers use a mathematical approach. Never build a stand-alone step. A single step creates a tripping hazard because it's difficult to see, especially at night and for people with limited vision. If you're considering using just one step, then you really should handle the elevation change with a sloped path. Use a minimum of two steps; three is better. As with paths, steps should be wider for a casual saunter through the garden, narrower for single-file access to a functional area. Make your steps a minimum of 4 feet wide, even wider if you want to stroll comfortably two abreast. Avoid using more than 19 risers in a single set of steps. If you need more than 19 steps to get to the top, break up the climb with a small landing halfway up (or every 19 steps if your garden extends up an especially long slope). Landings should be at least 4 feet long. Visitors appreciate a bench and a small diversion such as a pond or piece of artwork at a landing so that they have something to focus on while they catch their breath.

⬈ Originally, this backyard was a steep, forbidding incline. Now, a passage of stone, concrete, and turf opens up a new section of the yard.

⬈ Grass paths provide continuity to this three-tiered garden.

◀ Low, grassy steps can gracefully serve as an impromptu amphitheater where guests can perch.

auto access

The coming and going by car is a fundamental part of American life. Yet a home's auto access is often a neglected part of the landscape design, not neglected in the sense that it is not installed, but that it is not integrated with the yard, garden, and home. The driveway is typically a slab of unadorned concrete that runs straight to the garage or parking area.

▾ An aggregate concrete driveway interplanted with turf is higher maintenance than a solid paved surface, but it adds style and is good for the environment.

◂ This driveway of custom-made 3x5-foot pavers interplanted with Marathon grass sets the stage for an inviting dooryard garden.

Because the auto is how most people arrive at your home and most guests park in the first spot they see as they drive in, build a guest parking area, if possible, near the entrance you want visitors to use. Make getting from the parking area to the house a positive experience. If you want to leave no doubt in their minds which door to use, connect the parking and the entrance with an arbor or pergola and a path lined with colorful and inviting plantings.

Although it's important to provide autos with their own "garden rooms," there's a delicate balance between providing convenience and going overboard. Give no more than 9 percent of a property to auto access. This includes a driveway, parking pad, and turnaround. Informal studies have shown that any more than that leads to the impression that there is too much paving. Autos

require more room to maneuver than many people realize. Driveways need to be at least 10 feet wide and parking spaces need to be 10 to 12 feet wide and 20 to 23 feet long per vehicle. Square footage dedicated to autos adds up quickly.

Check with your local building inspector before installing a parking area. You must follow a number of rules regarding the setback from the street, the size of the paved area, the thickness of the paving, and the material used for the surface. Grass can offer an environmentally friendly parking solution that helps integrate your auto access with your lawn and garden. Precast concrete blocks can be filled with soil and seeded or plugged with grass. If you want a unique design, pour concrete and leave the forms in place so that you can later fill them with soil and plants. Make sure the soil is an inch or two below the surface so that grass blades have room to grow without being crushed by car tires.

Gravel driveways are attractive and good for the environment, but make sure they are approved in your community. Some areas have ordinances against parking on loose-stone surfaces to discourage people from tossing down a layer of gravel and parking on their front lawns. Other communities oppose hardscape paving because it leads to increased rain runoff, erosion, and depleted underground aquifers. You may be fined for paving too much surface area and then be forced to tear out some of it to meet code. Clearly, auto access is a big deal, so give it some thought.

▲ A good landscape design integrates automobile parking and access without allowing them to dominate the scene.

▼ The key to a successful driveway that integrates turf is to allow an inch between the soil and the surface of the concrete.

▲ Building a trellis screen
to camouflage an
air-conditioning unit is
an easy do-it-yourself
weekend project.

service areas

Somewhere in the deep recesses of your landscape are the ugly areas you'd rather forget about—the back alley, the air-conditioning unit, the pool equipment, the dog kennel, and the trash can storage area. Remember these areas in the design process. If you fail to set aside room for these necessities, you might place them into spaces that make them stick out like sore thumbs.

If you are building a new home, address these necessities during your site analysis. While building the deck, have the carpenters add a niche with doors to store the trash cans out of sight. Ask the contractor to pour a concrete pad for the noisy air-conditioning unit on the side of the house instead of on the edge of your secret meditation garden. You can add or move these items later, but it's more economical to think them through beforehand and get them right the first time.

Primary considerations in placement of service areas are accessibility, convenience, and screening from other areas of the yard. A firewood storage rack that is inaccessible will get little use. A clothesline distant from the laundry room will likely sit idle because the dryer in the laundry room will be much more convenient to use. Ideally, outdoor service areas should be located where you can naturally move from the indoor sections of the home with similar uses. So put that clothesline close to the laundry room and the firewood rack next to the family room with the fireplace. Include a permanent path between destinations to prevent soil compaction and dying turf if the area will receive frequent use.

Gathering service areas into one or two spots in the landscape will make more efficient use of limited space and make screening unsightly views associated with these ugly necessities of life an easier task to accomplish. Screening of scattered service areas may only draw more attention to the features you're trying to disguise.

Planners of neotraditional towns today are rediscovering the charm and practicality of the alley. Alleys—once considered dirty, dangerous places that had no place in the idyllic world of the new suburb—have much to offer the landscape. They allow parking to be placed behind the house and the front to be pedestrian-friendly. They give utility companies a place to hide all the wires and pipes that bring electricity, telephone service, gas, and water to homes and businesses. They also allow easy access to these modern conveniences for upgrades and repairs. The odor and noises associated with trash service can also be relegated to the alley, where they are less obtrusive.

◀ All it takes is a few tough plants to transform a seedy back alley into a dog-walking park.

▼ This magnificent alley in Richmond's Fan District is the result of one man's pass-along plants spilling over from his small garden.

veggies from asparagus to zucchini

A well-tended vegetable garden can blend nicely into the landscape, but more often than not, the broccoli, tomatoes, and other veggies are relegated to service-area status. As with any service-area feature, screening the element from view is a consideration. Hedges and privacy fences are the most common ways to hide an unsightly view. If designed well, the privacy fence could double as a barrier to bunnies and other critters that may compete with you for the tempting morsels in the garden.

When selecting the site for your vegetable garden, keep in mind the growing requirements of the vegetables. Most need full sun—at least six hours of direct sunlight a day—so avoid areas with a lot of shade. Vegetables also need good soil drainage. Raised beds may be a solution if the soil in your yard is poorly drained clay. Avoid low spots in the yard, not only because water will collect there, but, because these low spots tend to collect cold air, becoming frost pockets in spring and fall. A nearby outdoor water hydrant will make watering the garden easier during dry spells.

going in style

The first step in designing a successful landscape is to settle on a style that suits both your personality and your home's architecture. Are you a foursquare person with a symmetrical Federal-style home that begs for a formal topiary garden? Or are you a fly-by-the-seat-of-your-pants person with a quaint New England saltbox that calls for an informal cottage garden? You can certainly mix and match the elements from any of the various styles, but it is a good idea to have your design rooted in one style. While climate, sun exposure, soil, and many other factors vary, great gardens do share many elements.

basics of garden design

Whatever your aspirations, you should understand the basics of garden design. Once you recognize these basic building blocks, you can combine and use them to create your own unique landscape.

balance/symmetry

Achieving balance in a formal garden is usually as simple as having one side mirror the other. If you plant holly on one side of the walkway leading to the front door, plant the same size and variety of holly directly opposite it on the other side of the walkway. This straightforward method is a logical garden style for a home with a symmetrical design—a front door smack in the center, four windows upstairs, and four windows downstairs.

The design for an asymmetrical home with an informal garden isn't quite as straightforward.

▲ The colorful cottage garden to the right of the bench helps balance the visual weight of the wall on the left.

▶ A bonus in planning a symmetrical garden is once you've designed one side, you've essentially completed the plan.

One way to achieve balance is to coordinate the elements of size, number, texture, and color. For example, balance dozens of small, fine-texture plants on one side of a path by planting a few larger, coarse-texture plants on the other side. You can also balance a grouping of green plants with a few colorful ones. The weight distribution is perceived as equal, and the overall effect will have a natural, informal appearance that fits the architecture of your home. Don't force a formal plan on a house with asymmetrical architecture. Either move to another home, come up with an asymmetrical landscape plan, or limit the scope of formality in the garden.

▲ Large properties call for large features, such as a wide bridge spanning a big pond, massive plantings, and a spacious lawn.

◥ In this tiny train garden, pebbles become huge boulders, and ferns and a dwarf spruce are towering trees. It's all about scale.

▶ Most landscapes fall in the middle of the scale spectrum. Lawns should be the right size for the landscape.

scale

Scale is the relative size of one object when compared to another. While many aspects of garden design can be changed quickly and easily, the scale of a garden usually changes very slowly.

When it comes to scale, think of yourself as Goldilocks. You are the judge of whether something is too large, too small, or just right. If you have a grand five-story country manor, plan for a big lawn and plant trees and shrubs that will grow tall and anchor your home in the landscape. If you have a tiny seaside cottage, go with a small lawn, perennials, annuals, small trees, and shrubs, which will be easy to keep in scale with your home.

It is important to consider scale right from the start, because some things, such as the size of your lawn, the height of walls, and the square footage of your patio, can change only with a lot of time, effort, and money. On the other hand, it is possible for the scale of a garden to change over time without the gardener lifting a finger. If not kept in check with regular pruning, a boxwood hedge will have quite a different appearance 20 years after it's planted.

repetition/rhythm

The most straightforward principle of garden design is repetition. To master this concept, all you

⤷ Repetition in an undulating border has the power to draw visitors into the landscape.

▲ Columnar junipers and a strip of lawn serve as gracious garden-tour guides.

◄ These crabapples are spaced carefully to avoid future maintenance problems.

need to do is use the same element several times. If you've ever planted a hedge or created a border between your beds and lawn, you've used repetition. It can be subtle, such as a few containers along a path, or obvious, as with a row of trees planted at equal intervals along a driveway. A sequence of plants, pots, statues, or other elements can be an effective way to visually lead people to your front door.

Because perfectly spaced items rarely occur in nature, repetition is usually associated with formal gardens. It demonstrates the ability to manipulate nature. The real value of using repetition, however, is in giving a garden a sense of order. A backdrop

of tall evergreens unites mixed plantings in a border. And equal spacing of lobelias, candytufts, or other low edging plants at the front of a border brings order to a hodgepodge of plantings.

Before planting a hedge or formal allée, consult a knowledgeable nursery worker or reference book to determine the mature size of the plants. Keep in mind that close spacing increases competition between individual plants and may require extra watering and fertilizing. Close spacing also increases the risk of insect and disease problems developing on your plantings.

▸ Rows of shrubs framing the lawn create the illusion of greater depth and distance in this formal landscape.

▾ This elegant garden scene combines the elements of framing, repetition, balance, and perspective.

perspective

Although the concept of perspective is most evident in formal gardens, a hint of it can be used in an informal garden. A flowing naturalistic garden is always easy on the eyes, but a garden based on geometry can be equally appealing. In some ways, the simple lines created by straight paths, walls, pergolas, and hedges can be more tranquil than a jumble of plants and structures.

The perspective created by the way lines appear to converge in the distance leads you to explore farther down the line. Placing a focal point such as a fountain, urn, or other objet d'art at the end of the path or at the central axis draws visitors along the outdoor corridor.

Garden designers who want to make a small garden appear larger often use long sight lines to create an optical illusion. By making one end of a straight path slightly narrower than the other end, you can create a forced perspective. When this trick is used on a path that is narrower at the street and wider at the front door, your eyes will fool your brain into thinking the path is longer than it really is. If the path runs through the middle of your front yard, your lawn will look larger. It will have the opposite effect looking in the other direction, but this isn't necessarily a drawback. Looking down the gradually widening path from the sidewalk, your house will look closer to the street and, therefore, more friendly, approachable, and inviting.

framing

When you've painted a beautiful picture or snapped a great photograph, you want to frame it and display it for everyone to see. The same is true when you create a beautiful garden scene. Even if your scene is merely pleasant, creating a framework around it will often make it eye-catching and alluring.

Because it helps you focus, a frame can also be functional. If you want to steer visitors away from the side path leading to your laundry room and guide them to the front door, build an arbor, plant a pair of evergreens, or place a set of matching urns at the head of the path. Visitors will interpret these as arrows pointing the way. Frames also serve as welcome signs—a subtle way of marking an entrance, as if to say, "You've arrived."

Choose a frame that enhances your garden scene, taking clues from the architecture of your

► A bulky arbor draped with 'Cecile Brunner' roses frames an inviting garden scene.

◄ Border edging appears to converge in the distance. The circular fountain at the end draws your eye the full distance of the garden.

◄ Plants can be soft yet effective framing structures.

home and surroundings. To frame a path beside a large Tudor-style home, consider a bulky timber arbor that can hold its own with the grand scale of the home. To mark a trailhead or help weary visitors find a stone bench in a woodland landscape, a delicate rustic cedar arbor might be a more appropriate frame.

▸ Purple bellflowers and yellow loosestrife make ideal companions. They bloom simultaneously and their hues are opposites on the color wheel.

▸ Cool blues and greens produced by the blooms of Virginia bluebells and grape hyacinths bring a calming effect to the garden.

▸ 'Rustic Dwarf' rudbekia and 'Hot Bikini' helichrysum sizzle in a late-summer flower border.

▸▸ The bold tropical-garden style permits the use of vivid purples, pinks, reds, and yellows.

▸ If talk of color theory gives you a headache, take the easy way out and create a monochromatic garden. White is effective at night.

color

There are probably more theories on using color in the garden than there are weeds in your garden. Some gardeners prefer cool pastels, such as lemony yellows, soft pinks, and pale blues, which appear to recede and make the garden feel roomy. Others like it hot, hot, hot and fill their landscape with a riot of vivid red, orange, and school-bus yellow, which dominates the scene and makes a garden feel livelier.

Hue, value, saturation, brightness, tone, intensity—deciphering the mysteries of color coordination takes up volumes. Even if you want to create your own color theories, it's a good idea to study the color wheel and learn the rules before you break them. Consider the color of foliage, berries, bark, fall leaves, and winter twigs, as well as the color of your home, structures, paving, and outdoor furniture. If your patio bricks have pink and gray tones, plants with soft pink and purple tones will match best. If they are orange terra-cotta, pair them with yellows and greens. Feel free to experiment with color, trying different schemes in different garden rooms. Every approach is appropriate if it works for you.

▲ To plan a successful color scheme, one method is to use complementary colors, such as violet and yellow or blue and orange, opposites on the color wheel.

contrast

Contrast is one of the most effective weapons in the battle against boredom. When it comes to creating interesting plant relationships, opposites attract. Whether it's texture, color, scale, or shape, a little contrast brings life to a garden. One of the reasons lawns look so appealing is that their fine texture and light green color serve as a foil for the darker, coarser leaves and colorful blooms of nearby trees, shrubs, annuals, and perennials.

You can create a more dynamic garden by juxtaposing light and dark. Create a dark niche with an arbor or a grotto of thick evergreen yews and a trickling fountain beside an open, sunny lawn and watch how visitors are naturally drawn from sun to shade on a warm summer day. The reverse will be true on a cool afternoon in early spring, when you will flee the cold shadows in search of an open spot where you can bask in the warmth of the sun.

If you want to pair contrasting colors to create strong relationships, start by consulting the color wheel. Dark green and deep purple or burgundy on one side of the spectrum contrast with white, cream, and yellow on the other side. Variegated plants are appealing because the contrasting colors work well together.

Contrasting sizes and shapes make a more engaging garden. Throw in a mix of large, medium, and small plants. Varying the form of plants also creates contrast. Picture a tall, lanky Italian cypress beside a stocky 'Fat Albert' blue spruce surrounded by a sprawling mat of creeping junipers. The resulting combination is much more intriguing than three different plants with the same shape.

▸ Green is often overlooked in the color palette. Although it cultivates serenity, a green garden comes alive with texture and contrast.

▸ Remember to plan for winter. The golden glow of dormant zoysia bordered by green and gray lavender cotton provides exciting color contrast during the off-season.

▸ Contrast can also come from a can of paint. Painted structures, such as this pergola, bench, and fence, provide year-round accents to brighten the lush green foliage.

▸ This garden was laid out like a giant color wheel, with colors shifting from yellow to blue to purple to orange and red. A bright green lawn contrasts with a shaded patio.

texture

Texture is a wily way to bring depth and interest to a garden. By paying close attention to the elements of texture, you can create subtle optical illusions, as well as eye-popping combinations.

Bald cypress, dawn redwood, weeping willow, spireas, heavenly bamboo, junipers, boxwood, dill, rosemary, ferns, and ornamental grasses are all fine-textured plants. Coarse, large-leaf plants such as magnolia, sycamore, fatsia, palms, cannas, and hostas are at the other end of the spectrum. In the middle are plants such as maples, crabapples, azaleas, laurels, and gardenias.

Select some plants from each group to avoid a garden with too much of one texture. Too many fine-texture plants and your garden will come across as wispy and weak. Go heavy on the coarse plants and it will be overpowering. Remain neutral with only medium-textured foliage and it will blend together with nothing for the eye to focus on. The key is the right mix. You can hardly go wrong by using the florist's tried-and-true method of mixing round, spiky, and frilly plants in a single combination planting.

You can also use texture to alter the sense of depth. Because the eye perceives distant objects as small and hazy, you can make a small

▲ Spikes of cabbage palm and New Zealand flax are juxtaposed with more demure foliage.

◥ Even coarse-textured turf such as St. Augustinegrass appears refined compared to the monstrous foliage of philodendron nearby.

▶ It's hard to go wrong with a combination of roundy, spiky, and frilly plants.

garden appear larger by planting fine-textured, bluish-gray plants such as blue spruce, lavender cotton, and blue fescue toward the back. Make a large garden cozier by planting coarse green plants such as magnolias, hydrangeas, and palms in back.

design complexity

Garden design runs on a continuum—from simple to complicated. In the early stages of your design, decide where you want your garden to fall. Consider your personality as well as the amount of maintenance you want to pay for or perform yourself. If you're on the simple end, consider a large patio adorned with a few slow-growing plants in pots. If you desire more, you might wish to loll in your labyrinth garden filled with vegetables, hybrid tea roses, bonsai, and a pool.

Your garden should suit you and how much you like to garden. If you prefer clean lines and low maintenance, limit your wish list. A circular fire pit centered on a square terrace overlooking a rectangular lawn bordered by daylilies and an evergreen hedge of arborvitaes might be your ideal garden. If you want a vast perennial collection amid several cottage-garden rooms, your design will be more complicated.

Bite off only as much maintenance as you can manage, being careful to avoid monotony. Play it safe by designing your garden to be installed over time. Begin with a simple lawn surrounded by borders of groundcovers, unmortared bricks, or other edging that can be easily picked up and moved if or when you want to add a rose garden.

▲ In this yard, a straightforward, geometric design with a "floating" lawn, slate paving, trellis, pergola, and raised beds offers plenty to explore without being overwhelming.

◀ A lawn is vital to the design of busy gardens such as this one. It provides a spot that allows the eye to rest.

garden styles

formal style

Formal style conjures up images of stately pleasure grounds accented by vistas of grand parterres reigning over beds of roses, dramatic water features, geometric labyrinths, and fanciful topiaries. Formal gardens are epitomized by the Palace of Versailles outside Paris and the American estates of the Vanderbilts and Rockefellers, where the owners showcased their lavish use of land by creating these tightly designed, well-manicured gardens and lawns.

Although the high maintenance level a formal garden requires makes most homeowners shy away from this style, it is possible to borrow a few elements and scale them down to a manageable form that suits a more modest piece of property.

Instead of spacious parterres, add a series of raised beds for a modest *potager* garden just outside the kitchen door. You don't need a 5-mile-long approach to your home lined with 200-year-old live oaks to have an impressive allée.

You can plant a series of small trees such as redbuds, crabapples, or tea olives or shrubs such as boxwoods or arborvitaes along a narrow walkway leading to an arbor-covered swing at the back of your property. Halfway down the path, add a geometric fountain, a diamond-shape herb garden, or a matching pair of elegant urns. Featuring four-season statues on the corners of a small lawn is a simple way to make the lawn area more formal.

For a stately hedge that lends an air of elegance, plant trees or shrubs such as Leyland cypresses or arborvitaes that require little pruning to maintain their tight shapes. Be aware that when one tree in a hedge or allée dies, it creates a gaping hole that needs to be filled, often by a large, expensive, cumbersome replacement.

Well-designed and appropriately placed structures bring a sense of order to a garden. Build a refined gazebo that mimics an architectural element of your home and accent it with a simple reflecting pool. A bluestone patio surrounded by a tightly clipped boxwood hedge will tell visitors where to sit to enjoy the garden.

Creating a formal garden doesn't necessarily mean building a garden that triumphs over nature. Tap into your creative side and adapt the elements of symmetry, framing, sight lines, and repetition to create manageable garden rooms that suggest grandeur and opulence.

◀◀◀ Formal need not be stuffy. The unmistakable symmetry of this scene casually invites you to sit a spell.

◀◀ An armillary sphere surrounded by the silvery foliage of artemisia and lamb's-ears provides an elegant focal point.

◀ Water features in formal gardens are based on geometry rather than the free-flowing lines found in nature.

▸ This mowable edge makes maintenance easier because a string trimmer is needed only every four or five mowings.

▸▸ A tidy plot of turf brings order to a jumble of relaxed plantings and provides a cooler, more comfortable courtyard than solid paving does.

courtyard style

A courtyard is usually a limited-space garden that relies heavily on hardscape elements such as patios, paths, gazebos, walls, and garden sheds. Depending in which area of the country you live, these items will be made of different materials.

In the American Southwest, a courtyard is typically composed of adobe walls surrounding a hearth or chiminea and a tiled patio. Without water to support a large cultivated garden, it's best to wall off an area close to the house for planting and maintain it. Tile and adobe hardscape effectively hold in radiant heat to provide a few hours of comfortable temperatures after the sun sinks below the horizon. Drought-tolerant plantings, mainly natives, give the courtyard a lived-in look that harmonizes with the land beyond the walls.

Residents of the Southeast think of courtyards in terms of moss-covered brick walls enveloping a small geometric lawn bordered by palms, camellias, azaleas, tea olives, old-fashioned roses, and other sweet-scented flowers that invite owners and visitors to linger. A shady niche is an important element that extends the pleasurable hours in the hot, humid climate. A small wall fountain or splashing water feature provides the psychological calming effect of water. Wide brick or cobblestone edging surrounding the lawn provides a path to preserve the lawn from compaction from visitors viewing the garden or wheelbarrow-toting gardeners.

In small city courtyards, reflecting pools or fountains often double as spas, tiny plunge pools, or narrow lap pools. Arbors, trellises, walls, window boxes, balconies, downspouts, and any other well-anchored vertical structure become fair game as plant growing sites for spatially challenged gardeners. Vines and espaliered trees are particularly effective at softening the walls and ceilings of these outdoor rooms.

Innovative garden designers pull a few tricks to make a small courtyard feel larger. Adding mirrors on the back walls of arbors and pool houses fools the eye into thinking the garden goes on forever. Fine-textured foliage plants such as ferns, butterfly bush, and Japanese cedar planted at the far end of the garden give the illusion of distance. Because cool colors such as green, blue, and violet visually recede, placing them at the back of the garden also makes the space feel roomier.

Even gardeners not limited by property lines can make effective use of this style. Courtyard gardens restrict your garden area, allowing you to give over the remainder of your property to a lower-maintenance lawn, a meadow, or naturalistic planting.

⚡ A patchwork of grass- and concrete-filled rectangles provides an intriguing design. Tough bunchgrasses such as tall fescue work best because they hold up to foot traffic and don't grow runners that leap outside the confines of their allotted space.

◀ A pierced brick wall provides privacy yet allows passing breezes to circulate air for the health of plants and the comfort of people.

naturalistic style

A naturalistic garden is one that has been touched by human hands, however gently—an important distinction from a natural garden, which includes only plants native to the region. By using mainly indigenous flora and mimicking nature's planting plan, you can create a garden that promotes a connection with nature.

William Kent, an architect and painter, once said, "Nature abhors a straight line." With that statement, he began breaking down the fence between the garden and the English landscape in the 1730s. Even a curve can look unnatural, however. When you lay out that curvaceous lawn edging or that mulched path, avoid sharp, squiggling lines that appear without reason. Curves should follow natural topographical lines, which is why it's important to mark slopes on your site analysis map. As part of your gentle design, paths and streams should flow around trees, rocks, and other barriers.

Structures in a naturalistic garden could include a rustic arbor, a small stone patio, stepping-stones, log benches, free-form ponds, flowing streams, or even waterfalls. Plant selection depends on your personal preferences, but the idea is to take clues from the site. If you live in the southeastern United States and you are blessed with a wooded hillside of dappled shade, you

could choose Carolina hemlock and white oak with an understory of redbuds, dogwoods, Carolina silverbells, and sourwood. A mulched path winding around shrubs such as oakleaf hydrangea and mountain laurel surrounded by a carpet of wild ginger, partridgeberry, and trillium might be as far as you want to go.

To create a landscape you will enjoy, enhance the garden with well-behaved, introduced plants that grow well in your area and fit into your design. However, avoid planting invasive exotic plants that contribute to the detriment of native species. Contact your cooperative extension service for a list of plants that are invasive or illegal in your area.

▶ Although planted by human hands, sweeps of fountain grass, hibiscus, and purple *Perovskia* look like the work of nature.

▶▶ A harmonious symphony of giant feather grass, coreopsis, and other prairie plants softens the stony edge of this naturalistic garden.

◀ Purple coneflower, milkweed, and other wildflowers create an airy, low-maintenance prairie mix.

◀ You need only a small plot of land to create an effective wildflower patch.

▶ Black-eyed Susans are descendants of wild species native to virtually all of North America, so they are at home in almost any naturalistic garden.

✤ Although billowing borders are a hallmark of cottage gardens, an orderly patch of lawn is crucial for organizing the woody plantings.

▴ Spires of foxgloves are a must for any well-stocked cottage garden, and they attract hummingbirds.

cottage style

The soul of the cottage garden lies in its ability to achieve controlled chaos. A cottage garden in full bloom might appear to be a hodgepodge of plants, but if it's well-designed, there is a system to the tumbles of flowers and plantings. This romantic, carefree style developed in the late 1800s as a Victorian rebellion against harsh industrialization and the tidy landscapes created by gardeners of the Colonial period.

Flowers rule in the cottage garden—all shapes and colors of perennials, annuals, flowering shrubs, and small trees. The cottage garden is a great venue for the plant collector. Every available

An arbor, a bench, and a hint of stone path lend essential hardscape to these unbridled plantings.

When designing a cottage garden, gauge the size of the lawn by what you could mow with an old-fashioned reel mower even if you intend to use a lawn tractor or a self-propelled mower.

square inch is filled with plants, and there is always room for one more treasure.

Cottage gardens naturally lend themselves to time-tested plants associated with cherished memories of Grandmother's garden. Tall spires of hollyhocks, foxgloves, delphiniums, phloxes, and salvias mingle with frilly thrifts, verbenas, yarrows, and artemisias. Other favorite perennials include shasta daisies, lamb's-ears, columbines, irises, daylilies, coneflowers, black-eyed Susans, coreopsis, balloon flowers, and, of course, roses. Attractive fruits and vegetables such as strawberries, rhubarb, lettuce, cherry tomatoes, and vining gourds and peas festooning stick tepees or lattice trellises also find their way in. Mix in a few herbs for cooking, fragrance, or looks.

The profusion of plants leads some people to believe turf has no place in the cottage garden, but a little lawn is desired. A small clearing of lawn where you can place a couple of chairs or toss a ball with your kids, grandkids, or the family dog will prove valuable. A small lawn or a grassy path also provides much-needed contrast and allows the eye to rest from the onslaught of busy borders.

Like a sliver of lawn, the punctuation of a structure can provide valuable contrast and a focal point among the masses of plants. The structure can be as small and inexpensive as an eye-catching gazing globe, a sundial, or one-of-a-kind garden art. Larger, pricier structures such as arbors or gazebos that fit the romantic mood of the garden are also suitable. Fences, walls, hedges, and other enclosing structures are another mark of the well-appointed cottage garden.

▶ A drought-tolerant planting doesn't have to mean "zero-scaping." This garden under sunny New Mexican skies is exuberant yet water-thrifty.

southwestern style

Spanish explorers began colonizing what became the southwestern United States as far back as the 16th century. Five hundred years later, the charm and passion of the garden style of these early settlers still have influence on the region's landscape style, which has trickled to the rest of the country.

Spanish kings dictated strict methods for establishing their American colonies, including how to lay out public plazas and garden spaces. After taking care of the essential needs of shelter and food, colonists began mixing pleasure with necessity in their gardens. They used hardy plants, earth-tone paving, unpretentious metalwork, and rough-hewn woodwork to achieve a masterful blend of color, texture, and fragrance that seem married to the landscape. Palms, eucalyptus, junipers, bougainvillea, hibiscus, ornamental grasses, roses, cacti, agaves, and other succulents lend flamboyance but require little fuss to thrive in the region's harsh climatic conditions.

The drought conditions experienced in virtually all regions of the United States at one time or another over the past 20 years have caused the resurgence of the Southwestern style. With water at a premium, *Xeriscaping* has become the gardening buzzword as gardeners search for better ways to match their arid growing conditions with native, drought-tolerant plants. (For more on Xeriscaping, see page 126.)

The garden rooms of the Southwestern style are another key to its popularity. The Mediterranean influence of colonnades, cloisters, courtyards, terraces, patios, piazzas, verandas, and porticoes creates a host of opportunities to suit every mood of the homeowner. Whether you want to entertain your 500 closest friends on the piazza or slip away for a quiet read on a private balcony, you can create an alfresco gathering spot to suit the needs of you and your friends.

⚏ Low-maintenance elements such as succulents and gravel mulch combined with outdoor garden art in a courtyard setting have popularized the Southwestern garden style.

▲ Succulents such as this agave might shrivel under the stress of drought, but they recover quickly when watered.

◀ Forgoing aqua paint for their vanishing-edge pool, these homeowners selected a deep blue color to match the expansive Western sky.

◀ Fun and funky were the objectives of the designer of this garden. A checkerboard of recycled blue-glass gravel and baby's tears does the trick.

▶ A patch of turf provides the perfect outdoor gallery to display this humorous lawn art.

◀ The owner of this expressive garden in Oregon uses the space to display his own sculpture, a piece entitled *Silent Wind Chimes*.

urban style

Many urban gardeners struggle to harmonize the noise, traffic, and other mayhem of living in an urban environment. Urban gardens often celebrate the uniqueness of the individuals who create them. The gardens range from sophisticated, eccentric plots to comical settings filled with pink flamingos, whirligigs, toilet planters, and every other outlandish whatnot.

Some refer to this style as "shabby chic," and it's certainly true that recycling and creativity are important elements. Any item designated as weathered, distressed, antique, or retro plays well here. Using a little discretion, a lot of ingenuity, and perhaps a few yard sale finds, you can create a garden that has loads of personality. Hang old windows to enclose a deck, plant empty olive tins with herbs, or create a water garden from an old claw-foot tub with a showerhead water fountain.

Your neighbors are an important consideration in this style. Not everyone appreciates lawn edging fashioned out of retired bowling balls. You may want to consider a privacy fence or a thick evergreen hedge as part of your design.

When it comes to plant selection, think unstructured. Cannas, bananas, elephant's ears, and palms, inspired by the *tropicalismo* craze, are embraced by many urban gardeners. Annuals such as New Guinea impatiens, lantana, celosia, coleus, castor bean, and zinnias are good choices to mix in. Bold foliage and brassy blooms marry well with this garden style, but you can also fill your garden with clipped evergreen topiaries fashioned to resemble a herd of dinosaurs. Anything goes.

playing the hand you're dealt

Now that you have visions of your

Garden of Eden, it's time to consider such less-glamorous features such as clay soil, eroding hillsides, swampy ditches, and dry lawns. It's like a game of poker. You have to decide what to keep and what to throw away. You can convert that old dilapidated shed into a quaint potting shed or you can tear it down. You can turn that drainage ditch into a stony creek lined with birches, weeping willows, and hydrangeas, or you can replace it with buried pipes. Even if you have a new home on a lot scraped clean by bulldozers, you will probably have to deal with overhead power lines, neighboring property lines, or perhaps a slope. It's important to keep your ultimate garden design in mind, while working with what you have.

soil analysis

After the weather, the favorite topic of conversation among gardeners is soil. You can't change the weather, but you can change your soil. Start by analyzing your existing soil. After you know what you have, you can figure out what you should do to improve it.

soil tests

A Collect soil samples from several areas in your yard and at least 8 inches deep.

B Clay has a sticky texture, holds a fingerprint when damp, and remains intact when dropped from waist height.

C Loam drains well and has a deep brown color due to a good supply of organic matter.

D Sandy, gravelly soil allows nutrients to slip through easily, but it's easily amended with organic matter.

percolation test

A For a simplified percolation test, begin by digging a hole 8 to 12 inches deep.

B Fill the hole with water, allow the water to drain out, then fill the hole again.

C If it drains within an hour, you have good drainage. If it drains within six hours, drainage is moderate. Anything longer than six hours is in the poor range and should be amended.

Garden soil is composed of four basic ingredients: minerals, organic matter, water, and air. A good balance of all of these ingredients will lead to soil that is referred to as healthy loam. Inert minerals, ranging from large stones to sand to tiny clay particles, make up the largest part. Although they contribute few nutrients, they are an important part of soil texture. Nutrients come from decaying organic matter. Because the right balance of these four items rarely occurs in nature, chances are you'll need to help your soil along by adding fertilizer or organic amendments.

A soil test will tell you the soil's texture and pH and will offer recommendations for improvement. Contact your local extension office for information on testing soil professionally. You can also do a simple squeeze, or "ribbon," test to determine your soil texture. Take a moistened handful of soil and roll it between your thumb and forefinger. If it feels sticky and easily forms a ribbon longer than an inch, you have a high percentage of clay. Clay soil compacts easily, preventing salts and other elements from leaching out, causing a buildup that is harmful to plants. If your soil will not form a ribbon when pressed between your thumb and forefinger and it feels gritty, not sticky, when wet, you have sandy soil. Somewhere in the middle are desirable loam soils. A moist clump that feels gritty and slightly sticky but won't form a ribbon indicates a sandy loam. A clay loam will form a ribbon that is less than 1 inch.

While you can garden in clay or sandy soil, you can grow much more in good soil and grow it much better, so it's worth the effort to improve it. Even plants grown in healthy loam benefit from an annual application of organic matter or mulch and regular feeding.

soil improvement

Soil improvement is within the grasp of the homeowner. Most soil amendments are available in bags at your local garden centers. If you need large quantities, check garden centers, landscape contractors, or local classifieds for amendments sold in bulk. If you are unable to haul purchases yourself, most suppliers will deliver for a fee. Let your soil test guide your selection, but you can't go wrong with moderate amounts of organic matter.

▲ Forking over soil loosens it creating beneficial pore space for air and root penetration.

▲ A front-tine tiller is relatively easy to use. Use it to convert hard pan into friable soil.

soil amendments

Hundreds of soil amendments are available. Some are meant to improve general soil structure, and some are geared toward specific problems. Here are some of the major ones and what they can do for your soil:

• **grass clippings**—If you bag clippings, add them in small amounts to your beds or compost pile. Applied too thickly, grass clippings develop mildew and odor problems.

• **gypsum**—Often touted as a cure-all for heavy soils, gypsum improves aeration and drainage only when soils are also high in sodium, primarily in the West. Till or fork in as much as 350 pounds of gypsum per 1,000 square feet to improve the structure of salty clay soil.

• **leaf mold**—Ground-up, partially decomposed leaves are great for improving soil structure. They also attract earthworms, which aerate the soil as they move. Leaf mold does rob the soil of some nitrogen as it decomposes, so you may need to add fertilizer.

• **lime**—Lime raises pH, so use it to "sweeten" soil that is too acidic. Lime also adds calcium, important to plant vigor. Dolomitic limestone contains magnesium, beneficial for plants in small amounts. Hydrated lime, also called quicklime, dissolves quickly and can damage plants if not applied as directed.

• **manure**—Manure adds small amounts of nutrients. It must be well rotted so it doesn't burn plants. Composting reduces odor and weed seeds that may be present.

▲ leaf mold

• **peat**—Peat is partially decomposed remains of plants that have accumulated in oxygen-poor, water-saturated bogs. The most common element is decomposed sphagnum moss, but sedges and other organic matter are often included. Peat's ability to retain water and nutrients and improve soil structure makes it an ideal amendment for most soils.

• **sand**—When mixed with organic amendments such as peat, finely ground bark, or compost, sand can improve drainage. Do not add it to clay soils, however, or you'll end up with a soil more akin to concrete. Use coarse builder's sand, instead of fine play sand, which compacts easily.

• **sulfur**—A common way to lower soil pH (make it more acidic) is to add sulfur. High amounts can burn lawns and other plants, so be sure to follow product directions and measure accurately.

• **topsoil**—If your existing topsoil is thinner than a few inches and you are creating or patching a lawn, add topsoil. It should be tilled in so that no sudden shift occurs between the compacted subsoil and fluffy, new topsoil. If purchasing topsoil, make certain it is weed- and chemical-free. You might also consider "lawn soil," a sphagnum/ compost blend, instead of topsoil.

• **vermiculite and perlite**—These amendments are formed by heating minerals until they expand, forming lightweight and highly water-absorbent granules. Their porosity keeps oxygen in the soil. Although too costly to add to an entire lawn or large bed, they are practical for container gardening or potted plants.

taming a slope

Although most real estate agents would have you believe that the best kind of property is flat with lots of usable space, gentle slopes are desirable for their ability to drain excess water. They also add character to a landscape. Slopes, especially steep ones, do require some special consideration as you plan your landscape.

Generally, a grade of less than 30 percent (the ground rises 3 feet for every 10 feet of horizontal distance) is safe to cut with a lawn mower, so one option is to plant these slopes in lawn grasses. Always mow across a slope (not up and down) and be sure the grass is dry to avoid slipping. Dry grass also cuts more evenly. Use a string trimmer to roughly cut grassy hillsides.

Establishing turf on a slope is tricky. For small areas, sod is a wise option. Start at the top so that you don't slip on loose sod as you lay it, and run rows across the slope. Stagger seams to lock the pieces together. Hammer 4-inch-long dowels through the sod to hold it in place as it takes root. Remove the stakes after the sod has rooted.

▲ A dry-stack (without mortar) wall is an effective way to tame a slope.
1) Dig out the slope. 2) Lay a perforated drainpipe at the bottom.
3) Cover the pipe with landscape fabric and gravel. 4) Lay stones, angling them back into the slope. 5) Fill behind the stones with gravel as you build. 6) Finish by layerering landscape fabric, topsoil, and sod.

Seeding a steep slope often results in all your efforts slipping to the bottom of the hill. Seed gentle slopes and cover them with a biodegradable mulch, such as straw or burlap, to hold seeds in place until they germinate. On steep slopes, consider professional hydroseeding, in which a combination of seeds, paper mulch, and a glutinous adhesive is shot onto the hillside, where it sticks in place, allowing the seeds to germinate.

Another option for slopes is to plant a quick-spreading groundcover that will cover bare soil and prevent erosion. To help prevent weeds, retain moisture, and hold the soil in place as your groundcover fills in, mulch the soil well with pine straw, shredded bark, or other mulch that will cling to the slope. Use soaker hoses, drip lines, or perforated hoses that produce a fine spray to water new plantings. The impact of droplets shot from overhead sprinklers causes erosion.

If your slope is more than 30 percent, consider terracing it with retaining walls. Check with local building inspectors, but generally, garden walls higher than 4–6 feet require approval by a licensed civil engineer. Any wall—regardless of height—that holds soil around a home's foundation may require a building inspector's approval.

Do-it-yourselfers can tackle small, mortarless walls on gentle slopes. You'll find many preformed, interlocking, concrete-block retaining-wall systems on the market to make the task easier. Some feature a rough stonelike face or planting pockets that you can fill with soil and trailing plants to soften the look.

▸ One of the oldest uses for a wall is to bend the earth to human will. Here, a network of low retaining walls converted a steep slope into multilevel stages of usable lawns and gardens.

▲ Limb-up trees and select shade-tolerant turf to grow grass in your secret garden.

◥ A well-sited shade tree provides cool comfort for you, your plants, and your home.

▸ Quick shade provided by an elegant, vine-covered arbor encourages visitors to linger in the garden.

managing sun and shade

Achieving the perfect balance of sun and shade in the garden is an age-old dilemma. Homeowners with deep shade long for the warm rays of the sun to sustain their lawn grasses and the roses they desire. People with yards in full sun dream of a cool fescue lawn surrounded by shade-loving hostas. The ideal situation is to have some of both, so that you can suit every mood, guest, and temperature condition.

If your property is completely sunny, you'll want the comfort of a little shade. Trees are the natural choice. They filter pollutants and noise, produce flowers and fruits, change color with the seasons, and add water and oxygen to the air. Near your home, choose deciduous trees that will cool during summer and let in light and heat during winter. Plant smaller trees such as Japanese and amur maples, redbuds, crape myrtles, golden rain tree, and serviceberry near your home, and save the large evergreens and shade trees for areas farther removed so that they won't become hazards once they mature. Structures such as pergolas and arbors are good ways to get shade near the house. There are no tree roots to clog drains, leaves to clog gutters, or limbs to fall on your roof. Retractable awnings allow you to soak up the sun when you want it, and they provide instant shade on hot, sunny summer days.

If you have a tree-filled shady landscape, you may want to make some modifications that will allow you to soak up the warmth of the sun's rays. Simply "limbing-up" a few trees by pruning off lower branches at the trunk might give you all the sun you desire. If you're looking for more sunlight, check your site analysis (see page 30) for damaged trees that are good candidates for removal. If you have doubts or questions, call in a professional arborist. Before cutting, check for views you may not want to expose. You don't want to discover the trees you are removing were screening a view of your neighbor's old pontoon boat that now serves as a garden shed.

limbing-up

A telescoping pole saw/pruner allows you to remove dead or diseased branches or remove lower limbs to let more sunlight reach your lawn.

choosing a qualified arborist

Consider more than cost before hiring a professional tree trimmer. Start with these questions.

Are you a member of the National Arborist Association? Other legitimate organizations include the International Society of Arboriculture and the American Society of Consulting Arborists. Membership in these organizations comes with no guarantee, but at least it indicates that members are up on current tools and techniques.

Are you licensed? The trimmer should have a business license from the city or county in which he or she is based. If the person doesn't have a copy of the license or you're reluctant to ask, a call to the city hall or courthouse should verify its existence.

Are you bonded? This means that if the arborist accidentally fells a tree on your or a neighbor's house or damages anyone's property, you won't be stuck holding the bill.

Do you have medical insurance? Ask to see proof of insurance and follow up with a call to the insurer to make sure everything is current. Make certain the insurance covers everyone who will be working on your property.

Do you have references? Call references to see if the work was done on budget and on time. Give big bonus points for neatness. If possible, make site visits to nearby references so that you can look at the finished work.

Do you perform tree topping? If the answer is yes, you should run—not walk—away. Tree topping is the process of lopping off the ends of large branches, leaving stubs that don't heal properly. This leads to weak, suckering branches and makes the tree vulnerable to insects and disease. Unethical arborists perform tree topping in the hopes that you will call them back in a few years to cut down the now dead tree.

dealing with drainage

Even if you have fertile, loamy soil and the right mix of sun and shade, without proper drainage, it will all be for naught. You can correct some drainage problems with intelligent plant choices and soil amendments, but other situations require more elaborate solutions.

In areas away from the home, consider turning that slow-draining area into a bog garden. Bald cypress, hibiscus, Virginia sweetspire, canna, pitcher plant, Louisiana iris, and cardinal flower are attractive plants that tolerate wet conditions. If a bog garden doesn't appeal to you, install a dry bed of stones arranged to resemble a natural creek. Landscape it with birch trees, weeping willows, ferns, elephant's ears, and other water-loving plants and you will have an attractive feature.

You have several options for getting your plants up and out of damp soil. You can bring in topsoil to create a berm, a gently sculpted mound of earth.

installing a French drain

The French drain is a simple, easy-to-install drainage system that can save your lawn and plants and the foundation of your home from excess water.

Call to have your underground utilities located and marked.

1. Dig a trench approximately 10 inches deep, 8 inches wide, and as long as necessary to get the water out of the problem area. Make sure the bottom of the trench slopes away. About 3 inches of fall for every 10 feet of length is sufficient.
2. Fill the trench with 2–3 inches of gravel.
3. Lay 4-inch-wide lengths of pipe with perforated sides in

Swamp pinks, Japanese primrose, and creeping phlox converted this slow-draining area to a colorful bog garden.

Berms and swales solve water runoff problems by directing water away from home and plantings.

Don't fight storm water runoff with turf alone. Install a dry creek bed instead.

Whether you cover it with grass or larger plants, the key is to make it look natural with easy curves and no abrupt changes where new soil meets the existing grade. Another option is to build raised beds or use containers. You wouldn't want to place pots in a large bog in the center of your lawn, but in the right spot, they provide a viable alternative to slow-draining areas of gardens.

Options also exist for channeling water away from low areas. Swales are gently sculpted drainage easements that slowly carry water away, dispersing it as it goes and allowing it to soak back into the ground. If the swale isn't constantly wet, it can be planted with turfgrasses. If the swale stays soggy, stick with bog plants. If you just want to carry rainwater away from a downspout or prevent it from washing away your pea-gravel patio, consider a French drain (see below).

The answer to your drainage dilemma may be regrading—taking soil from high spots and filling in low spots. Whether you do this yourself with a wheelbarrow, shovel, rake, and keen eye or call in a professional with a bulldozer and surveyor's level depends on the severity of your problem. Keep in mind that you'll probably need to move more soil than you think.

the trench, placing the pipe holes to the side. Make sure the gravel you use is larger than the holes in the pipe, or it will clog the pipe. For extra insurance, wrap the pipe with a permeable landscape fabric (not plastic).

4. Cover the pipe with gravel.
5. Lay landscape fabric on top of the gravel the entire length of the pipe.
6. Fill in the top few inches with topsoil. If you intend to resod, allow an inch for the depth of the sod.
7. Top off the trench with sod or seed if it is located in the lawn or mulch if in the garden bed.

watering your lawnscape

Now that you've learned how to handle excess water, it's time to address getting water to your lawn and garden. To ensure your plants get the water they need in the proper amounts while using water wisely and efficiently, you'll want to take your time while choosing your tools.

in-ground irrigation

For most homeowners, watering conjures up images of knotted, leaking hoses; muddy shoes; and cheap, broken, plastic sprinklers—images that have had the in-ground irrigation industry booming for the last 20 years. Originally found only in large estate gardens, in-ground irrigation systems are now much easier to install and more affordable than they were during those early days of cast-iron pipes and welded fittings. They can also adapt to the needs of even the smallest courtyard garden. When designed and installed correctly, they ensure complete coverage custom-fitted to your landscape and the needs of your plants.

If you want to install your own in-ground irrigation system, do a little research first. Many local companies that sell irrigation systems have literature to help you. Some companies also offer design services for little or nothing if you buy the parts from them. If not, you can get design help (for a fee) from a landscaper or irrigation specialist. Several irrigation companies also have websites to help you plan your system.

the lowdown on in-ground irrigation

Whether you install your own in-ground irrigation system or you just want to ask an irrigation specialist intelligent questions, here are a few technique tips:

• Consider installing a separate line and water meter so that you don't reduce the water pressure in your home every time the system cycles on. A separate meter may also cut your water bill because some utility companies charge less for water that doesn't need to be treated as sewage.

• If you don't go with a separate line, make sure you have a backflow preventer to keep water in the sprinkler lines from siphoning back into the household water system.

• For most standard-size lawns, it pays to rent a motorized trencher to do the serious digging. You may also want a thin-blade trenching shovel for clean-out work and digging in tight spots. Remember, call the utility companies before you dig.

• After all lines are in place, but before installing any heads, run water through the lines to flush out dirt, pebbles, and PVC filings from sawed pipes.

• Unless you live in the tropics, install end caps at the lowest points of the irrigation system to drain water from the system during autumn to prevent ice damage.

• Include a moisture sensor that prevents your system from coming on when your landscape has had sufficient rainfall. One type works off a rain gauge and another measures soil moisture.

• Use high-pressure, schedule-40 PVC pipe for the main lines.

• To make final position adjustments easy and prevent accidental line breaks that often occur from bumping rigid PVC risers, use 3/8-inch flexible polyethylene tubing to connect all sprinkler heads.

Irrigation timer

- Modern controllers can be set to water different stations anytime you choose, but you have to learn how to program them. Some models feature a detachable panel with a battery so you can take it to a professional for help.

Funny pipe

- Flexible polyethelyne tubing (sometimes called "funny pipe") allows sprinkler heads to bend, rather than break when accidentally bumped.

High-pressure schedule 40-PVC pipe

- Schedule-40 PVC is the pipe of choice for in-ground irrigation. It's relatively inexpensive, lightweight, and easy to work with.

Backflow preventer

- A backflow preventer should be used with any landscape irrigation system to ensure that irrigation water isn't siphoned back into the potable water supply.

Pressure regulator

- Pressure regulators prevent fluctuations in water pressure that could damage irrigation systems or that could result in uneven coverage of irrigation water.

Irrigation filter

- A good filtration system will prevent debris and dirt from clogging drip irrigation or sprinkler systems.

Sprinkler head

- Installing pop-up heads in the lawn helps avoid damage from mowers. Risers in beds get water up and over surrounding shrubs.

⬆ To ensure even coverage, set sprinklers so that the spray from one head almost reaches adjacent heads.

▲ If you hire someone to install an irrigation system, select an established business and ask about references and guarantees.

portable systems

With new drought-resistant turf varieties and modern downsized landscapes, many homeowners can't justify the cost of an in-ground irrigation system. And some people enjoy the task of watering. It is a good opportunity to inspect plants for signs of insects, disease, weeds, lack of fertilizer, and other problems. The main complaint about portable irrigation systems is they don't last long. The key is to choose well-made products.

When it comes to gently showering young seedlings or giving a container of impatiens at the far end of the garden an emergency drink, it's hard to beat an old-fashioned watering can. Look for one that is lightweight and easy to use and has a spout that will provide an even, gentle stream of water to the plants.

A garden hose is probably the most important component of a portable irrigation system, and it's worth investing in a good one. Lengths generally range from 25 to 100 feet. Unless you have a small property, opt for the longer one. You'll find several options in diameter, materials, and couplings. The $1/2$-inch diameter is a bit small. The $3/4$-inch diameter hoses deliver the most volume and are less apt to kink, but they can be a bit heavy to drag around. The standard $5/8$-inch diameter hose is durable if you get one that is 5 or 6 plies thick. Rubber and vinyl are the two main material choices. Rubber costs a bit more but will last longer. The last major option is brass or plastic couplings. Brass lasts longer—often longer than the gardener who uses it does. In summary, dig a little deeper into your wallet and purchase a 50- to 100-foot long, $5/8$-inch diameter, 6-ply thick rubber hose with brass fittings that is backed by a lifetime guarantee.

the end of the line

When it comes to the business end of the hose, countless options exist, from copper-sculpture sprinklers to the homely old twisting brass-cylinder nozzle. Consider your plants and the design of your yard before you buy.

Nozzles that allow you to select a gentle shower, jet, mist, soaker, or angle spray are a great convenience. You can go from powerwashing mud from the wheel wells of your car to misting a tray of seedlings with a click. Look for a model composed mostly of metal rather than plastic.

Quick-link couplers allow you to add hoses and change nozzles in a snap. When you count all your spigots, hose ends, and nozzles, it can be a significant investment. Look for cost-effective starter packs containing several couplers.

Oscillating sprinklers are popular because their spray pattern conforms to the standard rectangular lawn. On better models, the arm will pause at each end of the sweep to compensate for the fact that the center receives twice as much water with each pass.

Revolving sprinklers have a rotating head that spins rapidly. Old cast-iron models in fanciful shapes such as alligators and frogs are fun to collect and great when the kids want to run through the spray on a hot day. The drawbacks are they tend to cover a limited area and they produce a fine mist that loses a lot of water to evaporation.

Impact or impulse sprinklers usually have a good throw radius and conform well to circular or oval areas. A spring-action arm breaks up a jet of water shooting from a revolving head. Based on time-tested agricultural sprinklers, these models distribute water uniformly with an entrancing, rhythmic pulse.

Traveling sprinklers, which usually look like little tractors, use water pressure to turn wheels that move them along a hose track. Revolving arms send out a uniform spray of water. The best models shut off automatically when they reach the end of the hose. They work great for large lawns but don't handle steep slopes well.

Fixed sprinklers have no moving parts, so little can go wrong. Most are relatively inexpensive, but pricier, decorative copper models you can leave in place all season are available. Their throw radius is limited, but they can provide a gentle spray to a limited area. Some have adjustable heads that allow you to select different distribution patterns. With circular, semicircular, linear, and even square patterns, a shape that will fit that odd little corner of lawn or garden probably exists.

⌃ Some fixed sprinklers have several settings for multiple spray patterns.

⌃ For a makeshift fixed sprinkler, wedge the end of a hose into the crook of a tool handle.

Garden hose
- To avoid frustration from kinks and tangles, and water and money down the drain, invest in a quality garden hose.

Rain gauge
- Use a rain guage to record the amount of rainfall you receive in your yard. Rainfall can vary greatly between your yard and the local weather station.

Timer
- When it comes to home irrigation system water timers, simpler is better. With a few strokes of the keypad, you can set the watering schedule for your entire yard.

Impact sprinkler
- The force of water shooting against the sprinkler head rotates the head in a circular pattern. They deliver a lot of water to a small area in a short period of time.

Oscillating sprinkler
- Oscillating sprinklers may be used in large open areas free of overhanging trees when air is still. They tend to deposit more water in the middle of their cycle of sweeping motion.

Traveling sprinkler
- Traveling sprinklers have a fairly uniform distribution. Take care when laying out the track of hose on which they travel to ensure all areas of the lawn are covered.

Circular sprinkler
- This fixed-spray sprinkler waters a circular pattern in the lawn. Evaporative loss of water is high because it has a high arching spray.

watering trees and shrubs

Trees and shrubs are typically the longest-lived elements of your landscape, providing you get them off to a good start. Proper planting (see page 129) is the all-important first step, but after that, irrigation is the most important chore.

The key to watering woody plants is to water deeply. Shallow watering leads to shallow roots unable to support the plant during dry periods. Make sure the area receiving water extends beyond the drip line of the plant, an imaginary circle on the ground where water drips from the branch tips. Roots of a plant extend well beyond this line. By watering in this area, you encourage the roots of newly planted trees and shrubs to grow and develop beyond the confines of the small original planting hole, leading to a healthier, more extensive root system.

Don't rely on lawn sprinklers meant to water only a few inches deep to adequately water a tree's entire root system. Drip irrigation is the most efficient way to get water to the roots of trees and shrubs. Disease-prone shrubs such as roses particularly appreciate a drip system, which doesn't spread diseases with each splashing droplet. A blast from an overhead sprinkler can also wreak havoc on the delicate blooms of flowering shrubs.

↗ Permanent high-rise sprinklers can shoot a spray of water over surrounding low-growing shrubs and perennials to reach distant areas in planting beds.

↗ Early morning watering is best. Watering at night can increase the likelihood of fungal diseases.

◀◀ A close up view of drip irrigation shows the water oozing from the hose.

◀ Although they require large volumes of water from a garden hose after planting, drip irrigation can effectively deliver water to trees as they settle in.

Another advantage of a drip system is that you can prescribe just the right amount of water for individual trees and shrubs. Use a small emitter head on shrubs and a larger one or more heads to provide large trees with plenty of water. The instruction manual that comes with your drip system should give advice on what size and how many heads to use on various sizes of plants.

You'll need to check a drip irrigation system periodically for signs of trouble. Wilted plants may be the result of a clogged emitter or tubing, and soggy ground might mean an emitter head has popped out or a line has been cut. Most drip systems come with a repair kit for splicing damaged hoses. Remember to add emitters or replace them with emitters that drip more gallons per hour as your plants get larger over the years.

Irrigation is impossible to plan according to the calendar. Although plants typically need more water during the heat of summer, be sure to check your plants year-round. If winter is windy and dry, plants may suffer drought stress, especially evergreens. Several inches of organic mulch around your trees and shrubs will help hold moisture in the soil, giving roots more time to soak it up.

Sometimes trees and shrubs go dormant during times of drought or after transplanting. If you discover a favorite tree has lost all of its foliage, scrape small sections of tender bark on the branches. If you spy a layer of green beneath the outermost layer of bark and the branch is pliable, the tree is still alive and does not need to be replaced immediately. It's also possible one branch is dead but the rest of the plant is fine. Give the dormant plant a thorough soaking, continue to water, and it just may make a comeback.

watering annuals and perennials

Whether you grow annuals, perennials, vegetables, or all three, they are most susceptible to drought stress at planting time. If the soil in the nursery container is dry, submerge the container in a bucket of water until air bubbles stop surfacing. After planting, thoroughly water the ground surrounding the plant. Water just the individual plants, and the surrounding dry soil will wick moisture away from the moist root ball.

The best method for watering established annuals and perennials depends on the design and the plants you've selected. For a handful of petunias in a window box, you might opt for the gentle shower delivered by the old-fashioned watering can. If you have a row of peppers in a vegetable garden or a long, narrow strip of impatiens at the front of a border, a soaker hose works well. Soaker hoses sweat water through their porous surface. When covered by a layer of mulch, they lose very little water to evaporation. It helps to stretch the hose out in the sun to make it more flexible before you set it in place. The main drawback with a soaker hose is that it loses pressure along the way, so plants toward the spigot end get more water than those at the end of the line.

Drip irrigation systems, which hold their pressure better along the entire length of line, are a good choice for these herbaceous plants. Although they work best with individual plants, some systems have bubblers that emit a gentle splatter of water that works well for groundcovers and other tight plantings. Drip systems can also be rigged to irrigate containers, including hanging baskets. Keep in mind that the combination of low water pressure and tiny openings means impurities can gum up the emitters. Filters and new turbulent-flow emitters that force water through tiny labyrinths cut down on clogs. Some systems allow you to deliver water-soluble fertilizer with each drip. If you go this route, make sure your drip system comes with a backflow preventer that will keep water and fertilizer from backing up into your drinking-water supply.

moisture sensors

Moisture sensors come in two basic forms—the rain gauge model and the soil moisture model. Both serve to conserve the earth's precious supply of clean water (and your money) by ensuring your landscape receives water only when it really needs it. As an added benefit, they extend the life of your system by preventing unneccessary wear and tear. Moisture sensors are wired to the system control panel and essentially short circuit it and disable it for the day when a reservoir determines there has been sufficient rainfall or a soil probe is still damp from the last watering. Old rain sensor models had to be physically emptied, but new ones are automatically vented and reset themselves.

◄ Soaker hoses can be hidden under a layer of mulch. They're great for hedges, rows of veggies, and plants on a slope.

▼ This drip system, available as a kit at home centers, allows you to place water at the base of individual plants. Less water is lost to evaporation and wasted on bare ground and weeds.

◄ It won't give your yard the look of an emerald carpet, but buffalograss is a very low maintenance grass for the High Plains. Improved cultivars include 'Comanche', 'Plains', 'Texoka', and 'Top Gun.'

a word to the water-wise

A portable lawn sprinkler puts out about 300 gallons of water per hour. Many residential yards receive several times that amount several times a week. Increasing populations and prolonged periods of drought have led to the increasing popularity of Xeriscaping, a new way of looking at water conservation in the landscape.

The term *Xeriscape* (pronounced zeer-uh-scayp), coined in Colorado in 1981, is derived from the ancient Greek word *xeros*, meaning "dry." The idea is to conserve water, time, and money by gardening shrewdly.

The first tenet of Xeriscaping is good design. Avoid sharp, awkward corners that make efficient irrigation difficult. You can easily end up wasting gallons of water on the sidewalk, patio, or street. It's also important to space plants properly. Plants too close together compete for moisture as they mature. Proper plant selection is important too. Don't try to grow water-gulping bog plants on a sunny slope. Plan for shade in your design to help your plants stay cooler. Grass and sun-loving perennials can tolerate a little high shade from trees that shield the high noon sun but let in the morning and late afternoon sunlight.

Xeriscaping divides your landscape into water-use zones. Set up high-, moderate-, and low-water-use zones by grouping plants with the same water needs. High-use zones consist of thirsty plants and sunny areas that require more water. A low-use zone could be a bed of drought-tolerant plants or the shady north side of the home. Water-use zones are also based on your expectations for the landscape. You can save a considerable amount of water if you let the grass in the backyard go dormant during drought conditions. You will have to accept a few more weeds, a lighter green color, and a lower-quality turf, but it's for a good cause.

Soil improvement is an important part of water-wise landscaping. By mixing in organic amendments, you'll improve the water-retention capabilities of sandy and clay soils. A topdressing of mulch on your beds helps hold in moisture and makes the ground cooler.

Conserve water by maintaining your landscape wisely. Water deeply. Check hoses and nozzles and repair or replace leaking parts. Sharp mower blades make cleaner cuts, which heal faster and lose less water to evaporation. Avoid fertilizing during extended dry periods, and when you do fertilize, select a slow-release product.

turf toughness

Turfgrasses are some of the most effective plants you can use when creating a water-wise landscape. Turf absorbs dust, filters pollutants, produces oxygen, and is a model of efficiency when it comes to reducing rainwater runoff and erosion. Here are some of the common turfgrasses and their drought tolerance. Check with your local extension agent to find out which particular variety performs best in your area.

most drought tolerant

Buffalograss : Bermudagrass : Zoysiagrass : Centipedegrass : Bahiagrass

native grasses

Whether you're interested in creating a natural lawn or a sweeping bed of wispy foils beside neatly trimmed turf, native grasses are an attractive, low-maintenance option. Here are a few grasses native to North America that are worthy of a spot in the cultivated landscape:

Grass	Height	Zones
Big bluestem (*Andropogon gerardii*)	8 ft.	4–9
Broom sedge (*Andropogon virginicus*)	3 ft.	6–9
Buffalograss (*Buchloe dactyloides*)	6 in.	3–9
Gray's sedge (*Carex grayi*)	3 ft.	3–8
Little bluestem (*Schizachyrium scoparium*)	3 ft.	3–9
Nodding feather grass (*Stipa cernua*)	2 ft.	8–9
Northern sea oats (*Chasmanthium latifolium*)	5 ft.	5–9
Pacific reed grass (*Calamagrostis nutkaensis*)	4 ft.	8–9
Prairie dropseed (*Sporobolus heterolepsis*)	2 ft.	3–9
Purple muhly (*Muhlenbergia filipes*)	2 ft.	7–9
Switch grass (*Panicum virgatum*)	7 ft.	5–9

⚡ Natural lawns can be beautiful, but keep in mind that they require weeding and reseeding like higher maintenance turfgrasses do.

◀ All plants need regular irrigation to become established, but mature plantings of cast-iron plants such as this 'Pfitzeriana Compacta' juniper can go months without water.

least drought **tolerant**

St. Augustinegrass : Fescue : Kentucky bluegrass : Perennial rygrass : Bentgrass

planting your landscape

From small packs of annuals tucked

into a window box to massive trees dug with hydraulic tree spades, a wide variety of plants are available for planting in the residential landscape. ⅏ You can begin the day with a bare yard and by sundown be gazing upon a blanket of green sod, cooling shade trees, foundation plantings, and cheery pots of petunias. ⅏ More likely, you are trying to stretch a modest budget to renovate a landscape that has both assets and liabilities. ⅏ You can gain satisfaction as well as save money by starting with seeds and smaller plants. ⅏ With thousands of types of trees, shrubs, annuals, and perennials available, you need not feel limited when selecting plants. ⅏ Use familiar, reliable plants for 75 percent of your selections, and include 25 percent new or unusual plants for a unique, personal look to your landscape. ⅏

start with the lawn

If you're a new homeowner, you have essentially two ways to achieve that new lawn you've always longed for—seed or sod. Seed offers the advantages of lower cost and a wider variety of grasses. Depending on the variety you select, you can seed a lawn for $10 to $20 per 1,000 square feet versus around $200 to sod the same-size area. The main investments will be your time and labor. The drawbacks of seeding are the time it takes for the grass to fill in and the ensuing battle with weeds in the meantime.

The big advantage of sod is obvious—instant lawn. Sod that is thick, healthy, and weed-free upon delivery means all you need to do is fertilize it and keep it moist until roots weave their way into the soil. Also, many of the refined cultivars of turf can be grown only by sod. Common Bermudagrass can be grown from seed, but the fine-textured 'Tifway' and 'Tifgreen' cultivars are produced only by sod or stolons. Zoysiagrass is also easy to grow as plugs (small cores of sod). For uniform germination its seed requires treatment to break dormancy. For this reason, its treated seed is expensive and difficult to find.

seeding a lawn

The first step in seeding a new lawn is to get rid of any existing vegetation and create a smooth, bare-dirt seedbed. An easy way to eliminate existing vegetation is to spray a nonselective herbicide such as Roundup® over the entire area. After about two weeks, most of the existing vegetation should be dead. Spray any persistent vegetation a second time and wait for it to die. You should be left with an expanse of browned-out grass and weeds. If your lawn is small, use a metal garden rake to roughen the dead turf. For large lawns, rent a power rake or vertical cutter and cultivate the entire area. This will remove much of the dead grass and thatch and help prepare that smooth, bare-dirt yard you need for sowing seeds.

Use a simple handheld or rolling spreader to sow seeds at the recommended rate. Spread a starter fertilizer to help your new grass seed establish faster. Press the seed into the soil with a pass of a roller. Cover the seeds with weed-free straw mulch (not weedy field hay) to hold in moisture and prevent erosion. Spread straw so that only about half of the bare soil is visible. Irrigate lightly but frequently at first; $1/4$-inch of water once or twice a day is enough. As grass fills out, gradually decrease the frequency of irrigation and increase the amount to encourage roots to grow deep into the soil. Keep traffic to a minimum the first few months while the tender grass becomes established. Feed with a good turf fertilizer one month after seeding.

seeding

Just like painting the walls of your home, 90 percent of the work involved with seeding a lawn is the prep work. To attain a quality lawn, you have to invest some time and energy in preparing the ground. The other critical step is selecting a quality seed of named cultivars that is fresh, and has a high germination rate and a low percentage of weed seeds and inert matter.

1. After killing the old lawn with a nonselective herbicide, till the area. To cut down on future weeds, rake the area, wait two weeks until new weeds sprout, and spray the area with herbicide again.

2. Rake the area to remove rocks and clumps of old turf.

3. Apply seed using either a drop or broadcast spreader. To prevent casting seed into nearby beds, patios, or paths, scatter by hand in tight spots.Use a rake to lightly scratch seeds into soil.

4. Apply a starter fertilizer to provide new seedlings with the nutrients they need for a healthy start. Starter fertilizers may also contain a weed preventer to suppress common annual weeds such as foxtail and crabgrass. (Make certain the weed preventer won't harm germination of the new grass you want to grow.) One month later apply a good turf fertilizer.

5. In confined areas, you can apply a floating row cover, burlap, or other light fabric to help hold in moisture. For larger areas, cover seed lightly with weed-free straw. Leave approximately 40–50 percent of bare ground visible.

6. Water seeded areas lightly and frequently to prevent tender seedlings from drying out. As grass grows, cut back on the frequency of watering and increase the volume.

7. Alternatively for slopes and large areas, professional hydroseeding might be an economical seeding option.

starting anew

Getting off to a good start means selecting the seed that's right for your situation. Many factors affect how grass will perform, but the main factor is sun exposure. Sun exposure is also difficult to alter, so it's important to select a mix that can thrive in your yard. You might need to use a sun mix in one section of the yard and a shade mix in another area or a mix developed for sun and shade.

overseeding an unhealthy lawn

If the health of your lawn is declining, and it has been adequately fertilized, overseeding might be the ticket to renewed vigor. If weeds are light (covering 10 percent or less of your lawn) and the soil drains well, you can simply spread the same or a similar variety of grass right into the existing lawn. It may help to introduce newer insect- and disease-resistant grasses or a type that is better-suited to the changing conditions of your yard, such as more sun or shade.

Late summer to early fall is the best time to overseed cool-season grasses in northern regions to give the grasses time to become established before they face the heat of summer or cold of winter. Late spring is best for warm-season grasses. Avoid the temptation to overseed too early in spring. The soil temperature several inches below the surface needs to be above 55 degrees for most grass seeds to germinate. Seeding too early results in increased losses due to freezing, erosion, or hungry birds. You should remove thatch (see page 164) before you overseed to help seeds make contact with the soil.

Overseeding will be ineffective if you have a serious weed problem (over 50 percent of the lawn is hard-to-control weeds). If this is the case, follow the "seeding a lawn" recommendations on page 130. If your lawn is less than 50 percent weeds, remove as many of the weeds as possible before overseeding. If your lawn weeds are annuals (e.g., crabgrass), apply a preemergence weed killer with fertilizer about two weeks before the weed seeds germinate in early spring. Most quality preemergence herbicides last three to four months, so applications must be timed so that the chemicals can run their course before any overseeding. Follow a recommended fertilization program through the summer, then determine whether overseeding is necessary in late summer.

winter overseeding

For some homeowners with a lawn of warm-season turf such as Bermuda-, zoysia-, or centipedegrass, the sight of a brown lawn all winter is disheartening. In areas with mild winters, it is possible to sow perennial ryegrass or rough bluegrass in fall to give your lawn a cheery, fluorescent green color through the dreary winter months. Fine fescue is also used for overseeding, but it may cause stiff competition for your warm-season turf come spring.

To overseed for winter, start by mowing the turf closely after it turns brown in fall. This gives the seeds a better chance to make contact with the soil. Overseed at nearly twice the rate recommended for seeding on bare soil because most of the seed will die before it finds its way through the thatch layer. Avoid casting seeds into nearby garden beds. A thorough soaking will help work seeds into the soil and spur germination within several days. Continue to irrigate through the winter if rainfall is insufficient. Mow late into fall and begin again in early spring. Overseeded grass will die off when temperatures heat up in spring and the existing warm-season grasses take over.

⬍ If your lawn looks anything like this, it might be time for a fresh start.

⚡ If turf is thin but relatively weed-free, you can revive it with a diligent program of aeration, fertilizing, overseeding, and selective herbicides.

▲ For winter overseeding with rye, you'll need to apply seed more heavily than when overseeding to renovate because much of the seed won't make contact with the soil below.

◀ Autumn leaves contrast with a lawn overseeded with perennial rye.

instant lawn with sod

As mentioned earlier, the big advantage of sod is obvious—instant lawn. You won't have to mess with a muddy or dusty yard for several weeks while seed becomes established. The main drawback is the cost. Laying heavy rolls of sod is no picnic either. If the cost of sodding the entire yard is too steep for your budget, one solution is to sod the most visible part of the yard, and seed the rest.

If your lawn is large, sodding is probably best left to professionals. If your lawn is a modest size, covering it with sod might be a doable weekend task. For comparison, get a couple of estimates from landscape contractors. Because they get sod at wholesale prices, you may find you won't save enough money doing it yourself to make it worth your time. Get the estimate in writing and check a few references before you commit.

▶ Sod comes in rolls or flat rectangles. The latter are lighter weight and easier to maneuver. Lay sod in a staggered pattern and butt seams together tightly to prevent edges from drying out.

◢ Sod is ideal for refurbishing high-traffic areas. Standing on boards as you work distributes your weight and prevents damage to the sod.

▼ To ensure you are getting a quality, weed-free sod, pay a visit to the sod farm to check out your potential purchase.

what about plugs and sprigs?

Plugs are small pieces of sod that are either cut from larger pieces or grown in plastic trays. Sprigs are bareroot grass. Due to their spreading nature, warm-season grasses such as Bermudagrass, Zoysiagrass, and St. Augustinegrass are the most popular types of turf planted by these methods.

Other than the one- to three-year waiting period required to achieve a solid lawn, the main disadvantage of sprigs and plugs is that they dry out and die easily if not watered diligently during establishment. You must also continue to battle weeds in the bare patches of soil as the turf spreads. Even with all their faults, you might consider plugs or sprigs if you are on a tight budget.

laying sod

The best time to lay sod for cool-season grasses is spring or early fall. Summer is feasible, especially for warm-season grasses, but you will have to irrigate diligently. Sodding in late fall or winter leaves the shallow-rooted sod susceptible to cold damage.

Do a little research before ordering sod. Inquire about the quality of the sod. Ask whether it is guaranteed to be reasonably free of weeds and diseases. Go a step further and ask permission to visit and check out the quality of the turf yourself.

Your soil should be weed-free and raked smooth (see seeding a lawn, pages 130–131) so that you can begin laying sod immediately after it arrives; sod left stacked on pallets in the hot sun will die quickly. Push the edges against each other firmly. Stagger the edges of the sod in a stair-step pattern to help prevent moisture loss around the edges and to lock the sod in place. This stair-step pattern will also help hold sod on slopes. Always run sod across hillsides. For steep slopes, use wire landscape pins or wooden dowels cut into 4-inch lengths and stuck into the sod to help it gain a foothold until roots are established.

You can use several tools to trim sod around beds, walks, and other obstacles. Some people prefer a long-handled edger or flat shovel with a sharp edge. Others prefer the precision cut of a utility knife used on the soil side of the sod. Avoid creating tiny pieces that dry out quickly. If you can't avoid them, pack the edges with a little topsoil to help keep them moist. Water immediately after the sod is in place, applying enough water to soak through the sod and 1 or 2 inches into the soil below.

▶ Water your new sod immediately after laying it. To encourage deep roots, be sure to apply enough water for it to soak through the sod and into the ground below. Starter fertilizer will get sod off to a quick start.

▶ Until new roots form, holding sod in place on a steep slope might require wire landscape pins stuck through the turf into the soil below.

▲ A half-moon edger with a sharp edge will help trim your new carpet of sod.

▸ A step-on edger does a nice job of trimming sod to fit along walkways, drives, or patios.

trees in the lawnscape

From the sprawling oak in the open lawn to the small Japanese tree lilac in a mixed border, trees are the most prominent and permanent plants on any property. They offer shapely silhouettes, foliage that changes with the seasons, colorful flowers, and intriguing bark. They frame homes, provide ceilings for gardens, and stir memories of people and places. On the practical side, they provide fruits for people, food and shelter for wildlife, and shade for homes, which lowers utility bills. They also reduce noise pollution, serve as windbreaks, and raise property values.

As desirable as trees are, plant no more than will comfortably fit on your property. Roots from trees too close together compete for water and nutrients, and crowded branches open the door for insects and diseases. Attempting to prune large branches away from your home, other trees, or utility lines often leads to an ugly liability. A better design calls for trees that fit the site and allow room for a diversity of other plants. Refer to your site analysis. You might love the bright, airy, open branches and papery bark of a river birch, but if you're shopping for a plant to screen the sights and sounds of a busy street, an evergreen with low branches and thick leaves would serve better.

Trees provide an important sense of scale for a home, establishing a relationship between people, architecture, and land. A property devoid of trees makes a home seem large and intimidating. When framed by mature trees, a home is brought down to a friendlier pedestrian scale. Large trees also fill the void of a vast, open property, making it appear smaller and more manageable. When planted at the back of a property, trees can make the entire yard appear larger. Specimen trees surrounded by lawn are fine, as long as they are protected by a generous ring of mulch to prevent damage from mowers and string trimmers.

Small trees planted near a home lend a friendly appearance, and they make a modest-size home look larger by comparison. This principle also works in the garden, where small trees make small garden rooms seem larger. Small trees can be part of the plantings near the home. For a lush, layered look that will also provide privacy, plant an understory of smaller trees such as dogwood, redbud, sourwood, winterberry, and serviceberry under large trees with high canopies.

shade-tolerant turf

Most grasses prefer full sun, but different types tolerate shade to varying degrees. Climate is also a factor. In northern regions, shade blends of Kentucky bluegrass and fescues work well in the shade. In the South, St. Augustinegrass is one of the best choices for shade. Mowing higher in shady areas gives the blades more surface area to absorb light. If you have evergreen trees or large deciduous trees that cast heavy shade, you should consider replacing lawn grasses with a shade-tolerant groundcover (see pages 148–151).

most shade tolerant

Fine fescue : St. Augustinegrass : Tall fescue : Perennial ryegrass : Kentucky bluegras

◀ Rather than treat trees as individual obstacles for your mower, combine them with shrubs and flowers in mulched planting beds.

▲ To prevent damage from mowers and string trimmers, surround individual trees in the lawn with a protective ring of organic mulch.

shopping for a tree

Before purchasing a tree, here are some questions you should have answered by a nursery employee, landscape designer, arborist, extension agent, or good reference book.

1. Is it deciduous or evergreen?
2. Is it rated for my growing zone?
3. What are its height and spread at maturity?
4. Is it a strong, hardy, long-lived tree?
5. Is it the best choice for the conditions of the site (light, moisture, soil, compaction, wind, salt spray, pollution, etc.)?
6. Will it serve my needs from a design perspective (screen, shade, color, winter interest, wildlife, texture, etc.)?
7. Are there any hardy, less-common varieties that would work for this situation?
8. Is it susceptible to certain insects or diseases?
9. Does it drop messy fruits, seeds, or other litter that could be a problem in some areas?
10. If this is a street tree, is it on the city's list of approved species?

least shade tolerant

Zoysiagrass : Bahiagrass : Centipedegrass : Buffalograss : Bermudagrass

▲ These rhododendrons are hand-pruned to maintain a relaxed shape and anchor the home without obscuring windows.

shrubs in the lawnscape

Trees may be the stars of the landscape, but shrubs are the hardworking supporting actors that make the stars shine. Shrubs form the walls between the carpet of grass, groundcovers, and paving and the support for the ceiling of trees and arbors. They provide shade for smaller plants, form low screens, attract wildlife, and bring fragrance and colorful flowers, fruits, and foliage to the landscape.

Although shrubs are a smaller investment than trees, you still should keep a few things in mind before planting. Learn a shrub's mature size before you plant it, remembering that it depends somewhat on growing conditions. Shrubs planted in ideal conditions will grow faster and larger than their counterparts grown under challenging conditions such as strong winds and clay soil. Where appropriate, plant a dwarf variety rather than struggle to keep a regular-size shrub small by excessive pruning. Keep in mind that flowers and fruits come and go in a matter of days, but the leaves are a long-term characteristic of most shrubs, especially when it comes to evergreens. Don't be swept away by the sight of a shrub in full

▸ It is possible to create an alluring landscape without colorful annuals and perennials. These beds are stocked with flowering trees and shrubs.

bloom at the nursery. Consider how it's going to look after the blossoms fade.

Shrubs are capable of performing many of the same practical duties as trees but on a smaller scale. Many can be used just as you would use a small tree—as a single specimen in a tight spot, mixed into a border, or as an understory beneath large deciduous trees. Sometimes the only difference between a small tree and a large shrub is the way the plant is pruned. Winterberry holly, viburnum, oleander, witch hazel, wax myrtle, and many other plants can serve in either way.

Most shrubs work best when paired with their own kind. Unless it's a rare beauty, a small shrub seldom makes an impressive specimen plant. Rather than scatter small shrubs here and there, plant enough in one area to make an impact.

Multiple shrubs of the same variety can be used to create hedges to screen a view, enclose a garden room, edge the lawn, form a backdrop for a border, mark a property line, or simply bring a formal, decorative element to the garden. First, select a shrub that lends itself to the type of hedge you want. Many shrubs make good candidates for loose, naturalistic hedges, but the list is shorter if you want a formal clipped hedge, limited mainly to slow-growing evergreens with small leaves. The second factor is proper pruning. Naturalistic hedges allow room for artistic interpretation. Prune a formal hedge so that the top is slightly narrower than the bottom. If you prune it vertically like a wall, the top hogs all the sunlight, resulting in a hedge that is thick at the top and sparse at the bottom.

shrubs for a clipped hedge

- Glossy abelia
  (*Abelia ×grandiflora*)
- Amur maple
  (*Acer ginnala*)
- Japanese barberry
  (*Berberis thunbergii*)
- Boxwoods
  (*Buxus* spp.)
- Peashrubs
  (*Caragana* spp.)
- Hedge cotoneaster
  (*Cotoneaster lucidus*)
- Box-leaf euonymus
  (*Euonymus japonica*
  'Microphylla')
- Rotunda holly
  (*Ilex cornuta* 'Rotunda')
- Japanese holly
  (*Ilex crenata*)
- Inkberry
  (*Ilex glabra*)
- Yaupon holly
  (*Ilex vomitoria*)
- Juniper
  (*Juniperus* spp.)
- Privets
  (*Ligustrum* spp.)
- Dwarf ninebark
  (*Physocarpus
  opulifolius* 'Nanus')
- Yews
  (*Taxus* spp.)
- Arborvitaes
  (*Thuja occidentalis*)
- American
  cranberrybush
  viburnum
  (*Viburnum trilobum*)

▲ It might not look like much now, but this row of small junipers will fill out quickly to provide an attractive, evergreen screen and effective windbreak. When planting a hedge, space plants properly to avoid crowding branches, which in turn leads to problems with pests and disease.

purchasing and planting trees and shrubs

The main options for buying trees and shrubs are bare-root, balled and burlapped, and container-grown. All three options have advantages and disadvantages.

bare-root

Bare-root plants have the soil removed from their roots and are packed in moist newspaper or sawdust. Mail-order suppliers prefer this method to reduce their shipping costs. Homeowners get the benefits of plants at perhaps half the cost of their container-grown counterparts. Fruit trees, cane fruits, roses, and flowering shrubs are likely candidates for bare-root. They should be shipped and planted only in winter and early spring while they are dormant. The disadvantage of bare-root plants is that only small plants are available. This is fine for roses, but if you want a large fruit or shade tree, you'll have to wait for it to grow.

When you get a bare-root plant, trim damaged stems and roots and soak roots overnight in a bucket of water. Dig a hole large enough to accommodate the roots without forcing them. Fill around the roots and water well. Pour a cup of water-soluble fertilizer solution around the plant.

balled and burlapped

Balled and burlapped (B and B, for short) trees and shrubs are grown in planting fields. Before shipping, the root ball is dug up and wrapped in burlap. The biggest advantage of this method is that you can purchase much larger plants than are available as bare-root or in containers. One drawback is that large plants can be extremely heavy. In most parts of the country, the ideal time for planting B and B trees and shrubs is fall or winter. Because most roots are severed when plants are dug, they need a dormant season when soil is cool, but not frozen, so that roots can grow. In cold climates, plant B and B plants in early spring. The planting season stretches through spring if you water regularly during summer.

B and B plants should be treated carefully. Support the root ball when carrying it. Don't use the trunk as a handle; the heavy root ball can pull away from the plant, severing roots in the process. Dropping the root ball can also damage the plant.

container-grown

The advantage of container-grown plants is that the entire root system is encompassed within the pot and no roots are lost when transplanting. Container plants can be planted any time soil is workable, although they need frequent watering if planted in summer. Lightweight pots make transporting tidy and convenient, and they are available in a wide range of sizes and prices. Before buying, pull a plant from its container and check the roots. A compacted, encircling mat of roots is a sign the tree or shrub should have been moved to a larger pot. Pot-bound plants struggle when planted, so it's best to pass on them. If the root ball pops out, leaving a lot of loose soil in the pot, the plant was probably recently moved to a larger container. It might not be worth the asking price because costs are normally based on container size rather than plant size.

With both container and B and B plants that have leafed out, wrap tops with a tarp, and take it slow when transporting them to avoid putting them through a hurricane-force wind.

proper planting of trees and shrubs

Planting a tree or shrub involves more than digging a hole. Here are the steps to follow to ensure you'll start your woody plant off right in its permanent home:

1. Place a tarp near the planting site to shovel the soil onto. Dig a hole twice as wide and a few inches shallower than the height of the root ball.

2. Place a long-handled tool across the planting hole. Check depth by placing the shovel in the hole and marking where the tool crosses the shovel.

3. Keeping your hand on the shovel, compare the depth of the hole against root ball height. If the hole is too deep, backfill and tamp soil. The root ball top should be 1–3 inches higher than ground level.

4. If soil is sandy or mostly clay, add compost or other soil amendments to the soil on the tarp and mix well.

5. For container-grown plants, gently scuff the root ball to help roots get a good start. Set the tree in the hole gently. For balled and burlapped trees, pull the burlap down so that it doesn't wick moisture away.

6. Backfill around the roots, gently tamping to make sure no large air pockets exist.

7. Tamp soil firmly around the root ball, using excess soil to form an encircling moat.

8. Water thoroughly. Follow label directions and apply a starter fertilizer solution around the plant. Continue to water every few days for the first month if weather is dry.

9. Add 2–4 inches of mulch, keeping it away from the trunk.

▲ A colorful mix of impatiens, ageratum, and begonias surrounds this lawn and breathes life into an otherwise austere landscape.

herbaceous plants

Without a doubt, most color and texture in the average landscape come from herbaceous plants—annuals, perennials, and bulbs. Considering their small stature, these plants carry serious visual weight. Even with the myriad options available, the list expands yearly as breeders introduce new and improved varieties. If you desire more than the options at your local nursery, add the thousands of varieties available by mail, and you will be astounded.

instant color from annuals

Annuals are plants that complete their life cycle in a year—from seed to plant to flower and back to seed. When planted in pots and beds in your garden, they provide brilliant floral displays that last several weeks to several months.

Annuals are usually purchased in small cell packs, but many are easily grown from seed. A $1.29 seed packet can bring thousands of blooms to your garden. And your investment isn't necessarily over when they die at the end of the season. Many readily self-seed, waiting for the right conditions to start the cycle again.

Because they produce so many blooms, annuals are heavy feeders that need slow-release fertilizer at planting time and biweekly applications of water-soluble plant food during the growing season. Deadheading spent blooms will keep plants tidy and encourage more blooms.

Use annuals to bring big impact to high-traffic areas such as entrances, around mailboxes, or on decks and patios. If you have limited space in beds, many annuals thrive in containers and hanging baskets. They also willingly fill gaps in borders until perennials fill out. If your landscape plan calls for a grand parterre rose garden in a prime location, but you need to build up your budget, annuals offer a great temporary solution.

Another benefit of annuals is their ability to accommodate your seasonal whims. If you later decide you don't like the variety you planted, you don't have to wait long before its time is up.

blooms on a budget

If you're looking for the most color for the least money, consider these annuals that grow easily from seed.

- Spider flower
  (Cleome hassleriana)
- Calliopsis
  (Coreopsis tinctoria)
- Cosmos
  (Cosmos bipinnatus)
- Globe amaranth
  (Gomphrena globosa)
- Sunflower
  (Helianthus annuus)
- Moonflower
  (Ipomoea alba)
- Morning glory
  (Ipomoea tricolor)
- Marigolds
  (Tagetes spp.)
- Nasturtium
  (Tropaeolum majus)
- Zinnia
  (Zinnia spp.)

◄ It's easy to coordinate simultaneous blooms when you select tireless bloomers such as coreopsis, 'Snow Queen' shasta daisies, sweet alyssum, and cosmos.

▼ This masterful mix of herbaceous perennials was carefully arranged by juxtaposing plants of various heights, colors, and textures. The lowest-growing, most-even green color and finest texture come from the lawn.

timeless beauty from perennials

Other than perennials' long life span, it's difficult to define this varied group of plants. They are typically herbaceous plants, but woody perennials also exist. Most go dormant during winter, dying back to their roots for several months, but some go dormant during the heat of summer. A few perennials are evergreen in warm climates. Some perennials have roots; others grow by rhizomes or bulbs. Most range from 2 to 4 feet tall, but ground huggers, such as ajuga and creeping raspberry, and giants, such as cannas and 10-foot-tall pampas grass, are also available.

Many people choose perennials because they want color in their garden without the chore of planting annuals each year. Most perennials require less maintenance than annuals in terms of planting, mulching, deadheading, fertilizing, and watering, but don't expect any to be maintenance-free. Some care, such as pruning, fertilizing, and mulching, can be done at the same time as an annual spring garden cleanup event. Most perennials, once established, require watering only during extended dry spells. Deadheading is beneficial for keeping plants neat and blooming longer, but it is not essential. The same goes for staking. The most taxing chore involved with

perennials is dividing them every few years when they become crowded. Use a garden fork to dig them up, separate crowded roots, and replant the divisions where they'll have room to grow for several more years. Or share the wealth of perennials with friends and neighbors.

Which perennials you choose depends on what you want from the plants. First, consider all of the usual cultural requirements. You need something that will handle shade or sun, wet or sandy soil, and the other conditions noted on your site analysis. Then you can consider aesthetic factors. Maybe you want flowers that offer great fragrance, attract hummingbirds, make good cut bouquets, or bloom all summer with minimum care.

You can take two approaches when designing with perennials. You can create a dynamite display by selecting plants that peak at the same time, or you can stretch it out to create a garden that has blooms coming and going all the time. It's difficult to achieve a landscape where numerous plants hit their stride at the same time. You can get bloom times from plant labels, but it's unlikely they will be more specific than early spring or late summer. Observing plants that are blooming in your area will give you some clues. Your design will look best if you plant groups of odd numbers and use drifts of the same variety to avoid the hodgepodge look. Repeat the drifts in other spots around the garden to tie different areas together.

⏫ Curved edging and ground-hugging plantings of ajuga and creeping phlox transformed this rock outcrop from a lawnmower liability to a graceful feature.

⏫ Perennial borders don't have to follow a formula. This motley combination of roses, lamb's-ears, iris, salvia and other perennials is unified by the lawn and path.

◀ A mixed summer border stocked with black-eyed Susans, salvia, flowering tobacco, and coral bells creates a jumble that is loosely based on arranging plants that step down in height.

ground control

For plants that can cover a lot of ground quickly and economically, it's tough to beat turfgrasses. Their fine texture, durability, and pleasant green color are inviting to the eye, and they set the stage for larger, showier plantings. However, no matter how much you irrigate, fertilize, aerate, and overseed, there are some areas where grass just isn't the best option. The site may be too shady for grass to grow or too steep to mow safely. Maybe your home is in a woodland setting, or perhaps you want to avoid the upkeep of a lawn mower. Groundcovers are grass alternatives that provide a similar, low-growing effect. By selecting the right plant for the job, you can turn a problem area into an attractive, low-maintenance carpet of color.

You will have an initial investment in establishing groundcover plants, but they will save you money and labor in the future. As you shop, select groundcovers with lots of roots and multiple crowns and divide them at planting time to help fill in the area faster. You will have to do some weeding as your groundcover fills in.

Consider sunlight, soil quality, slope, and other site conditions along with the qualities you want in your groundcover, such as color and texture of leaves, flower color, and season of bloom. Most groundcovers are evergreen, but you should be certain of this before you purchase a thousand plants. Also, keep in mind that groundcovers spread by several different methods. Many spread by underground stems, sending up shoots with new foliage as they progress. They perform best in loose soil, where runners can easily work their way through the top few inches. Other types are vines, crawling along the top of the ground, sending down roots as they go. Still other groundcovers are more akin to low-growing shrubs with a central trunk and branches that sprawl along the top of the ground. When planted properly, this type will thrive even if the surrounding soil is infertile and compacted, a benefit on a slope, where you want as little soil disturbance as possible to avoid erosion.

One of the most common areas to plant a groundcover is under a large tree, where lawn grasses struggle. You'll be disappointed if you simply chisel out a hole in the dry earth and plug in a few small plants. These tough conditions require prep work. The soil beneath trees is often compacted, but you should avoid tilling, which severs roots and stresses the tree. The best time to establish a groundcover is early spring, while the tree is dormant. Loosen the soil by irrigating the area and then use a manual garden fork to break up the ground. There's no need to turn the soil; just pry it up slightly to improve aeration. Avoid slicing or breaking any roots larger than the thickness of a pencil. Work in a 2-inch layer of compost or soil conditioner and then cover the area with a shallow layer (2 inches) of mulch. Piling on too much soil or mulch will smother the roots of the tree, depriving it of air, water, and nutrients. It's easier to plant the small groundcover plants through the mulch rather than adding it around the small plants afterward.

◀ Don't attempt to grow grass on dangerously steep slopes. Groundcovers such as lantana and agapanthus are a colorful and textural contrast to the turf.

◀ For this area in the deep shade of a deodar cedar, English ivy peforms better than turf would.

planting a liriope border

Liriope, or monkey grass, is a popular selection for living edging because it grows low and thick, spreads slowly, is drought tolerant, and has attractive foliage and blooms. Here's how to get it started:

1. Make the shape of your proposed edge with a hose. Using a shovel or small mattock, dig a trench. By digging a trench rather than single holes, you encourage the plants to spread in the direction of the trench.

2. Measure the length of your trench and purchase enough plugs (approximately 4-inch pots) to set one plant every 8-12 inches. Set them all out along the trench and adjust their spacing as needed.

3. Place the plants in the trench and cover the roots with soil. Water thoroughly. Rejuvenate plants annually by cutting them to the ground in late winter. Be sure to trim them before new growth appears.

1. carpet bugleweed

2. bearberry cotoneaster

3. wintercreeper euonymus

4. algerian ivy

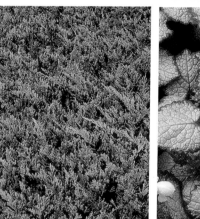

5. creeping juniper

6. spotted dead nettle

7. big blue lilyturf

8. mondo grass

9. japanese spurge

10. moss phlox

11. lavender cotton

12. dwarf bamboo

13. goldmoss sedum

14. creeping thyme

15. star jasmine

16. periwinkle

groundcover gallery
groundcovers for no-mow situations

1. carpet bugleweed
(*Ajuga reptans*)

zones: 3–9

height: 6 inches

description: Colorful evergreen, spreads by creeping stems. Many varieties offer mottled leaves of green, pink, burgundy, and cream. Spikes of blue or pink flowers in spring.

2. bearberry cotoneaster
(*Cotoneaster dammeri*)

zones: 5–8

height: 8 inches

description: Evergreen with long, stiff branches bearing small green leaves. White flowers borne in summer followed by showy red berries. Good on sunny, dry slopes.

3. wintercreeper euonymus (*Euonymus fortunei*)

zones: 5–9

height: 24 inches

description: Hardy vining evergreen with small, leathery leaves. Many varieties offer deep green, red, purple, and variegated white and gold leaves. Performs well in poor soil and full sun.

4. algerian ivy
(*Hedera algeriensis* or *H. canariensis*)

zones: 6–10

height: 12 inches

description: Evergreen vine with large, heart-shape leaves on maroon stalks, often variegated with creamy margins or centers. Not as unruly as English ivy. Best in light shade.

5. creeping juniper
(*Juniperus horizontalis*)

zones: 3–9

height: 12 inches

description: Sprawling evergreen with needle foliage in shades of blue to green. Most varieties take on purplish cast in winter. Covers quickly on dry, sunny slopes.

6. spotted dead nettle
(*Lamium maculatum*)

zones: 4–8

height: 8 inches

description: Medium-size green leaves mottled with silver. Vigorous choice to brighten dry, shady areas. Spikes of pink, purple, or white flowers in summer.

7. big blue lilyturf
(*Liriope muscari*)

zones: 6–10

height: 12 inches

description: Grasslike evergreen blades and spikes of purple or white flowers. Spreads by rhizomes. Easy to transplant. Good edging plant. *L. spicata* is smaller and more cold hardy (to Zone 5).

8. mondo grass
(*Ophiopogon japonicus*)

zones: 7–10

height: 12 inches

description: Similar to liriope, but smaller. Dark, evergreen; thin, grasslike blades. Grows slowly by underground rhizomes. 'Compactus' grows to 2 inches and is good for planting between pavers.

9. japanese spurge
(*Pachysandra terminalis*)

zones: 4–8

height: 12 inches

description: Soft stems with tufts of green leaves at tips. Great evergreen for shady areas under deciduous trees where fallen leaves disappear beneath the foliage.

10. moss phlox
(*Phlox subulata*)

zones: 3–8

height: 6 inches

description: Dense, mat-forming evergreen with tiny leaves, resembling moss. Produces a profusion of small, star-shape pink, violet, or white flowers in spring. Hardy in poor, dry soil in full sun. Needs no pruning.

11. lavender cotton
(*Santolina chamaecyparissus*)

zones: 6–9

height: 20 inches

description: Evergreen, dense mounds of silver, aromatic foliage and buttonlike yellow flowers in summer. Useful in poor, sandy soils. Does not tolerate damp, clay soils.

12. dwarf bamboo
(*Sasaella masumuneana*)

zones: 7–9

height: 3 feet

description: Evergreen, low, spreading bamboo. 'Albostriata' has leaves striped green and yellow. Best in compacted soil or areas surrounded by paving to keep it contained. Great variability in height, so be sure to select a dwarf form.

13. goldmoss sedum
(*Sedum acre*)

zones: 4–9

height: 2 inches

description: Tough, mat-forming evergreen with abundant yellow, star-shape flowers. Good in well-drained alkaline soils in full sun. 'Aureum' has bright yellow leaves.

14. creeping thyme
(*Thymus praecox*)

zones: 4–9

height: 2–12 inches

description: Most are mat-forming, aromatic plants that spread by trailing stems. Good for planting in crevices. Tolerate some foot traffic. 'Elfin' and 'Minimus' form dense, 2-inch-tall clumps.

15. star jasmine
(*Trachelospermum jasminoides*)

zones: 7–10

height: 12 inches

description: Tough, evergreen twining vine with dark green, glossy leaves and small, creamy, fragrant summer flowers. Prefers fertile, well-drained soil and protection from cold and full sun.

16. periwinkle
(*Vinca minor*)

zones: 4–9

height: 6 inches

description: Vining evergreen with small, oval, glossy, dark green leaves. Produces pale purple flowers in spring. Diminutive, well-behaved alternative to *Vinca major*. Best in rich, well-drained soil under trees or along shaded banks.

pulling
it all together

When trees and shrubs are mixed with perennials, groundcovers, and annuals, you can achieve a balanced landscape design that offers something inviting year-round. By carefully selecting plants you like that fit the growing conditions of your property with a minimum of pampering, you will have a landscape you will enjoy with little effort.

Most homeowners want to put their best face forward, so the front yard is a good place to start. Concentrate your efforts on a design that anchors your home yet is welcoming to guests and visitors. Your landscape plantings should

▼ To anchor a low foundation without covering up windows or a porch, select vertically challenged plants such as Annabelle hydrangea, astilbe, and lady's mantle.

blend the vertical walls of your house with the horizontal plane of the ground in a scale and style that complements the architecture of your home. A three-story home on a large lot calls for a generously proportioned lawn and beds that will hold several layers of plants. A small, single-story cottage on a tight property would look better with narrow beds filled with small shrubs and colorful perennials. Garden plantings should highlight the front walk and draw visitors into your home. Unless you are trying to direct visitors away from

◀ Specimen plants such as a dwarf Japanese maple belong out front, where they will receive the most admiration. When possible, place them by a window to be enjoyed from inside as well.

▼ Even in a tight spot, there's room for a combination of shrubs, annuals, and perennials. The trick is to limit your palette and still achieve a variety of color and texture.

▲ A generously proportioned planting bed was used here to balance the grand scale of this 2-story corner. As the plants fill out, they will shelter this stark side of the home and direct attention to the front door.

a shortcut, avoid thorny plants, especially those that will crowd paths or steps.

It's important to make your garden beds look good from the street, but don't neglect the view from inside. You don't want to be stuck looking at the back side of plantings. Rather than planting all the tallest plants at the back and stepping down like a grade-school class photo, mix the plantings up a little. You also don't want to block the view from windows, so consider the placement and mature sizes of foundation plants.

Large, windowless walls and corners of the house are good areas to use taller plants. Use them to frame windows and anchor the house, but don't plant them so close to the house that they will cause problems as they grow. Don't try to convince yourself that you can keep a large plant in check with regular pruning. Enough good plants are available that you need not settle for a bad choice that will create extra work or result in an unnaturally shaped plant. Look for ways to interweave plantings to make beds attractive from all angles. This strategy might mean using

evergreen groundcovers and smaller plants that will grow beneath and behind larger trees and shrubs. Hostas, astilbes, ferns, and other low-maintenance shade plants are perfect for dressing up shady niches beneath or behind larger plants.

Another consideration is the off-season. Most of the United States lies within a temperate climate where winters force many plants into dormancy. If your yard is planted exclusively with tropicals or perennials that are dormant from November until April, your home will lack the friendly support of plants for nearly half of the year. On the other hand, yards filled with evergreens and a hardscape miss out on the changing of the seasons. A basic backdrop of evergreens fronted by a mix of deciduous shrubs and flowering perennials will give you the best of both worlds.

▲ These front yard plantings envelop the home with an appealing combination of vibrant annuals and soothing green conifers.

◄ Neatly trimmed evergreens anchor this foundation year-round, while the pansies provide springtime color and extend a cheery welcome right up to the front porch.

caring for your lawnscape

Once you've achieved the landscape of your dreams, it's important to make time for regular preventive maintenance to avoid serious problems later. ⺁ Many homeowners fertilize the grass when it turns pale green, prune the shrubs when they're covering the living room window, and spray the dandelions when they notice seed tufts blowing across the lawn like a summer snowstorm. ⺁ A better approach is to maintain a schedule that will keep your lawnscape healthy, rather than correct problems as they arise. ⺁ It's the same logic that tells you it's worth spending a little time and money on an occasional oil change for your car to avoid spending serious money on a new engine down the road. ⺁

lawn maintenance

▲ For small yards and out-of-the-way patches of lawn that are difficult to access with a larger machine, the reel mower is handy, reliable, inexpensive, and neighbors will appreciate the sound of silence.

A well-maintained lawn sets the tone for the rest of the yard. You may have stately trees and beautifully blooming perennials, but no one is going to notice them if they're fronted by a pitifully thin carpet of weed-choked lawn interspersed with bare patches.

making the cut

Mowing tops the list when it comes to lawn maintenance. From the first warm days of spring until the fading warmth of fall, Americans are out mowing their lawns—which is fine, because lawn grasses are meant to be mown. The grasses that have survived as turf are the ones that recover quickly from regular shearing.

When done correctly, mowing is the best thing you can do for your lawn. When done improperly, it can be the worst thing you can do. Follow two simple guidelines for proper mowing. First, follow the rule of thirds—remove no more than one-third of the length of the grass blades with a single mowing. Second, mow at the upper range of the recommended height for your grass type. If you don't know what type of turf you have or if yours is not listed below consult a local extension agent or the Scotts "Identify Your Grass" tool at www.scotts.com.

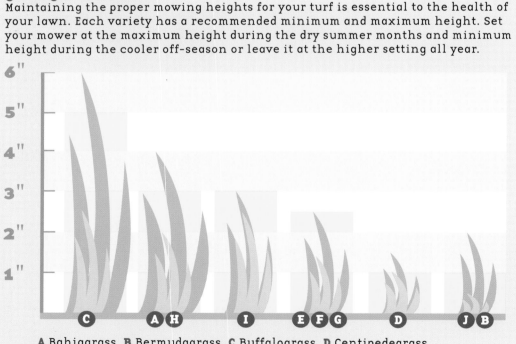

grass growth chart

Maintaining the proper mowing heights for your turf is essential to the health of your lawn. Each variety has a recommended minimum and maximum height. Set your mower at the maximum height during the dry summer months and minimum height during the cooler off-season or leave it at the higher setting all year.

A Bahiagrass, **B** Bermudagrass, **C** Buffalograss, **D** Centipedegrass, **E** Fine fescue, **F** Kentucky bluegrass, **G** Perennial ryegrass, **H** St. Augustinegrass, **I** Tall fescue, **J** Zoysiagrass

the right mower for you

Selecting the best mower doesn't mean choosing the biggest, shiniest model with the most horsepower. You need one that fits you and your lawn. Here are some types of mowers and how they stack up:

A Reel

Features: Consider this simple machine if your lawn is less than 2,000 square feet. Yes, they're still being manufactured.

Pros: Few moving parts to maintain, quiet and inexpensive, good for the environment and for aerobic exercise. Multiple reels can be mounted to a frame and pulled by a lawn tractor or ATV to cut a wide swath.

Cons: Narrow cutting width (typically 20 inches). Hard to cut thick turf such as zoysiagrass or tall grass, so you need to cut often.

B Electric

Features: Best for lawns less than 5,000 square feet. Cordless models with rechargeable batteries are an improvement over corded models.

Pros: Quiet, environmentally friendly, and easy to maintain.

Cons: Easy to run over the cord (always start nearest the outlet and mow away). Corded models may reach only 100 feet from the outlet. Limited mowing time before recharging required.

C Gas walk-behinds

Features: Mowing deck typically 20–22 inches. Walk-behinds work well for ½ acre or less. Newer models offer lower noise levels, mulching capability, fuel efficiency, and reduced emissions. Look for mulching models with easy-to-adjust deck height.

Pros: Good exercise. Good for moderate slopes and tight spots (caster wheels are a plus). Mulching models return nutrient-rich clippings to the soil without clumps. Relatively inexpensive ($300–$900).

Cons: Most are noisy. Require regular maintenance.

D Lawn tractors

Features: Good if you have more than an acre to mow and other garden chores. Typically have a front-mounted engine, lots of horsepower (12–20 hp), and a wide mowing deck (38–48 inches).

Pros: Versatile. Wide mowing deck. Many attachments such as dozer blades, snow throwers, utility carts, and grass-catcher carts.

Cons: Need storage space. Heavy, so they compact soil and use more gas. Expensive to maintain and purchase ($1,000–$5,000). Noisy.

E Riding

Features: Best for lawns between ½ and 3 acres. Generally range from 8.5 hp to 14 hp with mowing decks 27–38 inches wide.

Pros: Make quick work of most suburban lawns. Many models offer zero turning radius. Less expensive than lawn tractors ($1,000–$2,500).

Cons: Not as durable or as many attachments as lawn tractors. Noisy.

F Robotic

Features: Stays within the confines of lawn edging or buried cable. Some use solar power; others use a rechargeable battery, which can be recharged on its charging station when it runs low.

Pros: No physical labor. Quiet. Fun to watch.

Cons: Expensive (around $1,500). Cut randomly, so you don't get cleanly mown strips. Watch for curious kids and mower thieves.

◀ On older mowers, deck height is adjusted with a wrench. Newer models are easily adjusted without tools.

mowing right

Mowing the lawn during the heat of the summer may be one of your least favorite chores. Still, avoid the temptation to drop the mower blade height too far, thinking you won't have to mow again for three weeks. Cutting off too much of the grass blade exposes tender stems to sun rays, which leads to problems down the road. Avoid cutting off more than one-third of the blade in a single mowing. If you've come home from vacation to a 6-inch tall lawn, cut it back gradually. Cut off an inch or so, give the grass several days to recover, lower the blade, then mow it again.

Uneven spots in your lawn are susceptible to damage from scalping, a condition that opens up spots that weeds assume you created just for them. Continuous scalping will lead to a deterioration in the quality of your outdoor carpet. If you have bumps, holes, or sharp dips, shave them down or fill them with topsoil.

An improperly balanced mower blade can also cause scalping, resulting in a greenstrip (mown at the proper height) next to a brown (scalped) strip. To fix this problem, replace the blade or balance it by shaving a bit of weight off the heavy side so that it will rest on the level. Hardware stores offer balancing kits to help with this task.

Keeping the mower blade sharp is important in maintaining healthy grass. If you notice a brown cast to your lawn, inspect the grass blades. If they have jagged brown tips, it's time to sharpen your blade. Remove the blade and check for cracks or deep nicks. A metal grinder is handy for sharpening your mower blade, but you can also do it with a metal file.

mowing tips

A A scalped lawn can result when the mower deck is set too low or from an unbalanced blade.

B To avoid unsightly, jagged brown tips that lose precious moisture, sharpen mower blades several times per season.

C Without a protective ring of mulch, this young camphor tree was cut down in its prime by brutal string trimmers and careless mowers.

D Mulch preserves the protective layer of bark on tender young trees.

the finishing touch

Mowing your lawn just right is like having your hair cut for a nice, neat appearance. Shaggy edges where the lawn meets paved areas or planting beds can spoil the entire scene. Maintaining manicured edges around trees, beds, sidewalks, patios, and driveways gives your yard that finishing touch.

A good landscape design will cut back on the time you'll need to spend spot-trimming your lawn. You'll do yourself a big favor by creating smooth edges that your mower can maneuver around with one pass. A continuous edge of a thick, slow-growing groundcover such as liriope or mondo grass is an option around garden beds. Mulching and planting at the base of fences, walls, and trees will help those areas.

String trimmers are the usual tools of choice for edging, with both gas-powered and electric models available. Electric trimmers are relatively quiet, and there's no gas to mix or engine to maintain, but if you have areas to edge that are farther than 100 feet from an outlet, you'll need the freedom of a battery-powered or gas model. Avoid connecting multiple extension cords to allow you to edge more than 100 feet away. An extension cord reduces the voltage to the unit and can burn out the motor. Trimmers powered by rechargeable batteries free you from the tether of the extension cord and the upkeep of a gas engine, but if you have a lot of ground to cover, they can run out of juice before you get the job done.

It's likely that string trimmers cause more damage to the American landscape than any other lawn tool, with trees the primary victims. The only thing that frightens a tree more than the sight of a hard metal mower deck headed straight for its thin-skinned trunk is the whizzing blur of a nylon string trimmer edging ever closer. The simple solution is to add rings of mulch around the bases of lawn trees. You still may need to use the trimmer to maintain a neat edge where mulch meets turf, but the trunk will remain safe. Another option is to group trees and shrubs to create island beds with curving edges. Before you create the bed, outline it with a garden hose and make a test run with your mower, with the blade disengaged, to make sure you can mow along the edge in one pass.

Another option for creating neat edges is the old-fashioned edger. This sharp, metal half-moon with a handle slices a clean line along turf edges. Shop around for a sturdy model that won't break at the base of the handle. Maintain a sharp edge on the tool with a file or sharpening stone. Edging while the soil is moist will make this chore easier and improve your results. Step edgers provide a new twist on this old favorite. Because you place your foot in a stirrup and walk along the edge, you get better leverage as you throw your weight into it. A handlebar at the top of the tool also helps, allowing you to pull it out of the soil with both hands.

trimming along paved surfaces

String trimmers are great for cutting encroaching turf along driveways and other paved surfaces. A neat cut requires some practice. Safety glasses are always important, particularly when the trimmer is tipped to cut vertically.

watering your lawn

Unless you're a shaman with the power to summon the rain spirits to your yard on a weekly basis, you will have to water your lawn at some point. The various irrigation options are discussed on pages 118–121. Once you've decided on a system, it's a matter of using it properly.

For starters, water early in the morning so that grass has time to dry out before the cooler evening. Grass blades that remain wet for long periods are more susceptible to fungal diseases. It's fine to occasionally give your lawn an emergency drink in the early evening, but if you do it consistently, you're asking for trouble. However, in the Southwest, where low humidity, desiccating winds, and high summer daytime temperatures can evaporate moisture quickly, it is better to water in the evening. Just keep a keen eye out for any signs of diseases and switch back to a morning routine if you see any problems.

Another key to irrigating your lawn is making sure your system is delivering the proper amount of water. It's important to water deeply and not too often. Water needs to reach about 8 inches deep into the root zone, which usually takes about an inch of water per week. Watering less leads to a lawn with a shallow root system that doesn't survive extended dry spells.

Although not as common as too little water, too much water can also be a problem, depleting oxygen in the soil and creating a breeding ground for diseases. Constantly soggy soil is great for bog plants, but it's not the way to maintain a healthy lawn. Most types of turf are content with $1/2$ to 1 inch of water applied once or twice a week. Many weeks this may come from rainfall, which is why it's a good idea for an automated system to have a

▲ A simple rain gauge set in the lawn is the best way to check the volume of water your lawn receives from precipitation and irrigation.

▲ Portable sprinklers are inexpensive and convenient, but the amount of water delivered is unpredictable and distribution is uneven.

▲ A control panel allows your in-ground irrigation system to tend itself. Keep your instruction booklet handy.

rain gauge that keeps the system off when it's not needed. Even if you don't have an automated system, a rain gauge can help you determine if you need to run your sprinkler to make up for a shortage that week.

Even if your irrigation system was professionally installed, you should check occasionally to see if it is delivering adequate amounts of water (see "Tin Can Alley" below). If you find a problem with water pressure, volume, or coverage and can't remedy it yourself, call in professionals who can conduct an "irrigation water audit." They will take readings of hydraulic data such as the pounds per square inch (psi) of pressure in your system, flow rates (volume in gallons), sprinkler distribution uniformity, and the infiltration rate of your soil. Make sure they also give you a usable translation of all this data, such as "You have a leaking pipe here" or "You need an extra head here." Infiltration rates are important because if your sprinklers are delivering water faster than your soil can absorb it, you will lose water through runoff. If your soil is high in clay content or on a slope, you may need to set your timer to cycle the sprinklers on and off several times to allow the soil time to absorb enough water.

It's easy to check the volume of water with a drip system. Because emitters are gauged in gallons per hour, you can simply put the head in an empty gallon jug, check your watch, and see how long it takes to fill. If it fills in 15 minutes, you are delivering 4 gallons per hour. Check the guide that came with your kit to ensure you are delivering a reasonable amount of water for the size of the plant. It's easy to forget about drip tubing buried under a layer of mulch. Leave the emitter heads just above ground so that you can find them easily and check them regularly for clogs. Also, be sure to clean your system filter periodically.

tin can alley

Whether you irrigate your lawn with an automated in-ground system or a thumb placed over the hose nozzle, here's a way to see if your system is delivering the proper volume and distribution of water.

Randomly set several 12-ounce metal cans in your lawn. Any container with straight sides and deep enough to prevent water loss due to splashing will work.

Let your sprinkler run for 20 minutes.

Measure the amount of water in the cans (e.g., 1/4 inch).

Divide 1 inch by the amount in the can (1 ÷ 1/4 = 4).

Multiply the results by 20 minutes (4 × 20 = 80).

In this example, you will need to run the sprinkler for 80 minutes to deliver an inch of water.

163

a breath of fresh air

Most people know how essential oxygen is to humans, but they rarely consider it as vital to plants. Roots need air for the plant to thrive. Kids and pets playing on the lawn, the mail carrier taking a shortcut, and you and your lawn mower all compact soil. As your lawn is trod on, soil particles are compressed and air is forced out. Compaction also prevents water and nutrients from entering the soil. You can spot compacted areas by the puddles left after a rain. When water does finally sink into compacted soil, it's slow to drain out, leading to waterlogged soil with even less oxygen.

Compaction also contributes to thatch buildup because compacted soils lack the oxygen needed by microorganisms that break down thatch. To determine whether your lawn has too much thatch, cut out a small section of sod with a knife or spade. If the thatch layer is more than $1/2$ inch thick, it's time to aerate. Aeration allows air, water, and nutrients to penetrate thatch and reach the roots of your grass. In many cases, aerating will cure a thatch problem, and you can avoid dethatching, which is harsh on a lawn. If you have sandy soil, which does not compact easily, aeration may be one garden chore you rarely need to perform. If you have clay soil, you may need to aerate annually. It's particularly beneficial on sloping lawns, where water may run off faster than it can soak in.

In vegetable gardens and planting beds, you can fork or till soil to get air down to the root zone. When it comes to lawns, it's another matter. You can aerate a lawn two ways—manually or by machine. Whichever method you choose, it's essential to aerate when the soil is moist. If it's too wet or too dry, the aeration won't be effective. The tines need to reach several inches into the soil, so a light sprinkling of water won't be sufficient. A deep watering is needed.

Several tempting gadgets, such as strap-on spiked shoes, claim to aerate while you stroll across the lawn. To do the job right, however, you need a core aerator with hollow metal tines that remove small plugs of soil 2 to 3 inches long and $1/2$ inch in diameter. If you have a small lawn and lots of energy, use a hand aerator, which has a long handle attached to a horizontal bar with two or three metal corers. Stepping on the bar forces the corers into the soil and removes plugs of soil when you pull the aerator out. Use power core aerators for large lawns. With hollow tines on a spinning drum, these machines can cover a lot of ground quickly. Their main drawback is that they are heavy and cumbersome, making them difficult to maneuver if used on a small lawn and to transport from the equipment rental shop. You may want to consider hiring a professional.

▲ Aeration effectively prevents thatch buildup. The process is a bit harsh on grass, so do it when turf is actively growing and when heat is not excessive.

↘ Plugs removed by core aerators will decompose quickly and act as a lawn topdressing.

▸ A manual core aerator is good to have in your arsenal of tools. Even if your lawn is so large it warrants a power aerator, a manual one is perfect for compacted paths and other high-traffic areas that need attention more often.

⇥ Thatch develops when organic matter accumulates faster than microbes, earthworms, and other organisms can break it down. If a sample reveals more than $1/2$ inch of thatch, use a core aerator to pull plugs of soil.

weed wars

Weeds are truly the bane of a gardener's existence, and controlling them involves a battle plan that meets the enemy on several fronts. The most effective control is to create conditions favorable for growing a thick, healthy lawn that won't allow weeds to gain a foothold. Do this by proper fertilization, irrigation, aeration, and mowing. If your lawn is more than 50 percent hard-to-control weeds, it may be more efficient to spray a nonselective herbicide such as Roundup®, till, and start over with sod or seed (pages 130–137).

Weeds may be classified into groups that have traits in common. Weeds in a group can often be controlled with the same methods. One such grouping is the separation into grassy weeds (monocots) and broadleaf weeds (dicots). Another basic division of weeds is into annuals and perennials. Perennials live for several growing seasons. Annuals can be futher divided into winter and summer annuals. Summer annual weeds germinate from seed as weather warms in the spring and die with the first frost of fall. Crabgrass is a summer annual. A few annual weeds die with the first hot weather of summer. These are called winter annuals. Their seeds usually germinate with the first cooling weather of fall; plants live through the winter, form seeds in spring, then die in hot weather. Annual bluegrass is an example.

Mowing at a high setting helps to control annual weeds becasue the grass is a strong competitor that may prevent weed seeds from germinating. However, if the lawn is thin, you may need to use preemergence herbicides. These are compounds that kill germinating seedlings but don't harm established plants.

▲ A lawn with more than 50 percent difficult-to-control weeds, such as violets or undesireable perennial grasses, is easier to replace than to revive.

▲ Dandelions in a lawn are easy to control with preemergence and selective postemergence herbicides, paired with fertilizer to strengthen turf.

Perennial weeds can be more difficult to control than annual weeds. Since perennial weeds survive from year to year, keeping their seeds from germinating isn't enough to control them. Perennial grassy weeds are the most difficult to control. Any control method you use on them will also affect the lawn because they are similar to lawn grasses.

The best weed control is a well-fed, thick, healthy turf. Properly managed grass out-competes most weeds. Mow high to help shade out weeds. Fertilize following the schedule on the back of the fertilizer bag. Watering mature turf deeply and infrequently (at least $1/2$ inch twice weekly) is best. Fall aeration discourages weeds by opening the soil so grass grows more strongly.

Pulling or digging weeds works well with some weeds, especially if there are only a few. For hand pulling or digging to be effective, frequent careful inspections are necessary, and you must pull every weed that starts, being sure to remove the root.

herbicides demystified

Chemicals that kill plants are called herbicides. The terminology on those bottles and bags of herbicides can be daunting. Two basic types of herbicides exist, each with its own action and method of use.

• Postemergence herbicide
Kills weeds that have already sprouted. This form of herbicide may be either contact or systemic; selective or nonselective.

• Contact herbicide
An herbicide that kills only the plant parts it comes in contact with. Works quickly, but weeds often resprout from underground roots or bulbs that aren't touched.

• Systemic herbicide
The chemical moves through all parts of the plant, including roots so all parts of the plant including the roots are killed by a systemic.

• Selective herbicide
Kills particular types of plants without harming others. The most common ones used in lawns—the ones contained in weed-and-feed fertilizers—kill broadleaf weeds but not lawn grasses.

• Nonselective herbicide
Kills any vegetation it is applied to, including grass. Sold as ready-to-use sprays or as concentrates. Roundup® is the most popular herbicide in this group.

• Preemergence herbicide
Kills weed seeds as they germinate. Effective against annual weeds. Should not be used in lawn areas you intend to overseed soon.

• Active ingredient
The chemical that controls the weed. Usually a small percentage of the material in the container.

• Inert ingredient
The harmless material used to help spread the active ingredient at the proper rate.

• Weed and feed
A blend of a lawn fertilizer and a selective herbicide.

▲ Nonselective herbicides kill all plants they contact. Control the direction of spray with an adjustable nozzle and spray only when the wind is calm.

▲ These three products are weed-and-feed blends. Bonus S is used primarily in the south on St. Augustinegrass. Turf Builder Plus 2 controls dandelions and other broadleaf weeds on most lawns, but shouldn't be used on St. Augustinegrass. Winterizer Plus 2 controls dandelions while preparing the grass for winter. Always read and follow label directions for use.

1. brown patch

2. dollar spot

3. fairy ring

4. fusarium blight

5. necrotic ring spot

6. powdery mildew

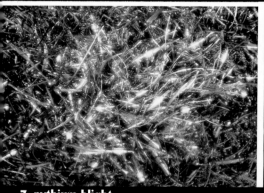

7. pythium blight

8. red thread

9. rust

10. summer patch

A healthy residential landscape supports an incredible number and diversity of life-forms. Just as some plants earn the label "weed" because they are unattractive, in the wrong place, and crowd out something more desirable, members of the animal kingdom become pests for similar reasons. Healthy plants can take a little nibbling from a few pests, so it's important to fertilize, irrigate, amend soil, and do all the things that give your plants an advantage over pests. Determine what kind of enemy you're dealing with and then find an effective control. Treat diseases with a fungicide only after an accurate diagnosis has been made and you have incorporated the cultural practices necessary for a healthy lawn. Indiscriminate spraying of pesticides will waste money and may kill beneficial insects that prey on the harmful insects. Here are some of the more common lawn problems and advice on how to deal with them.

diseases

1. brown patch

Profile: Common lawn disease that often appears after several days of rain.

Damage: Large brown patches surrounded by dark purplish halos in the morning. Minor outbreaks may affect only tender new growth at the blade tips. Severe cases kill the grass with the patches, which allows weeds to crop up.

Control: Avoid overwatering and watering at night. Treat with a contact fungicide and continue each week as long as hot, humid weather continues.

2. dollar spot

Profile: Occurs most often during periods of moist, mild days and cool nights.

Damage: Round, light brown patches start out about the size of a silver dollar or softball.

Control: Avoid walking in infected areas and spreading the disease to healthy grass. Water in the morning, and don't overwater. Apply fertilizer. If the problem persists, treat with a fungicide.

3. fairy ring

Profile: This mysterious circle of mushrooms appears overnight in areas with acidic soil where an old tree stump or other wood lays buried. The fungus grows out from a central point, and mushrooms crop up when weather conditions are right.

Damage: Not particularly damaging, but it is unsightly, and its thick network of underground growth can compete with grass for water.

Control: Pick the mushrooms before they release spores, then discard them. Aerate, fertilize, and irrigate. Fungicides won't help.

4. fusarium blight

Profile: Soil-borne disease that attacks some varieties of Kentucky bluegrass.

Damage: Small gray-green patches appear in hot, dry, windy conditions commonly found in the Midwest and West. Patches grow outward as grass wilts and dies. Weeds often take over the center of the patch.

Control: Irrigate regularly and apply lawn fertilizer at appropriate times. Treat with a systemic fungicide and overseed with a resistant cultivar of Kentucky bluegrass, fine fescue, or ryegrass.

5. necrotic ring spot

Profile: Appears in spring and fall when conditions are cool and wet but subsides in warm weather. Typically attacks cool-season grasses in the Northeast and Northwest.

Damage: Circular spots of light brown or red begin at 6 inches, enlarging to several feet in diameter and may merge to create large blighted areas.

Control: Aerate, dethatch, and fertilize regularly and irrigate in summer.

6. powdery mildew

Profile: Whitish to light gray fungus appears when days are warm and humid and nights are cool and damp. Typically found on Kentucky bluegrass, fescues, and Bermudagrass, especially in shade.

Damage: New growth may be stunted and distorted. Severe cases may weaken grass, making it susceptible to other pests.

Control: Reduce irrigation and improve sun exposure and air circulation if possible. Treat with several applications of a systemic fungicide and reseed thin areas with resistant cultivars or shade-tolerant grasses.

7. pythium blight

Profile: Fast-acting, waterborne fungus that attacks ryegrass and other cool-season grasses when they are scalped, heat-stressed, or poorly drained.

Damage: Irregular, 1- to 4-inch diameter spots of wilted, light brown grass that expand rapidly. Infected blades mat together when stepped on. Fine, cottonlike threads visible on blades before dew dries.

Control: Avoid walking in blighted areas. Treat with a contact fungicide specifically geared toward pythium blight. Infected areas may die within 24 hours and require reseeding in fall.

8. red thread

Profile: Light tan to pinkish webs appear in round patches during cool, wet weather.

Damage: Not a serious threat to lawns because it doesn't affect roots, but it can be unsightly and may indicate a nutrient deficiency.

Control: Apply fertilizer.

9. rust

Profile: Powdery orange substance brought on by warm, moist weather and nitrogen deficiency.

Damage: Lawn turns reddish brown, thins out, and succumbs easily to winter damage.

Control: Treat with a systemic fungicide, remove clippings, and fertilize.

10. summer patch

Profile: Similar to necrotic ring spot, except symptoms appear in summer.

Damage: Infects grass roots during cool spring weather, but turf patches turn brown when hot, dry weather stresses the grass.

Control: Apply a systemic fungicide and reseed affected areas with a resistant variety in fall.

1. ants

2. aphids

3. armyworms

4. billbugs

5. chinch bugs

6. cutworms

7. Bermudagrass mite damage

8. mole crickets

9. sod webworms

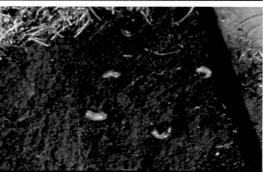

10. white grubs

insect pests

Insects' natural pathogens and predators, such as bacteria and nematodes, are sometimes considered as alternatives to chemical pesticides. However, several problems limit their practical use on lawns. First, most are more expensive than traditional pesticides. Second, biological controls tend to be highly selective, only attacking one stage of one species of pest. Third, it is difficult to keep these materials alive long enough to be effective.

Today's insecticides are generally either pyrethrum derivatives or insect growth regulators (IGRs.) Insecticides derived from pyrethrum, a natural product from a chrysanthemum-like flower, include pyrethrins and synthetic pyrethroids. Insect growth regulators interfere with insect development rather than kill pests directly.

1. ants

Profile: Many species of ants abound in the United States, ranging in size and color combinations of black, red, and brown.

Damage: The fire ant, with its stinging bite, is the no. 1 ant enemy of people. They also girdle fruit trees to get sap and build unsightly mounds in lawns. Other ants actually encourage aphids on your plants so they that can dine on the sticky honeydew they secrete. Carpenter ants may hollow out trees and invade homes.

Control: Many insecticides on the market are designed to treat fire ant mounds. Combine mound treatment with regular application of a product that treats the entire lawn to prevent the fire ants from moving to another section of the yard. Phorid flies, natural enemies of fire ant, are being imported and tested as a control.

2. aphids

Profile: These $\frac{1}{16}$-inch-long, pear-shape, soft-bodied green bugs are more commonly associated with roses and other flowers, but some also affect lawns.

Damage: Although small, a single blade of grass may carry dozens of aphids, all sucking the juices from it. The bronze, dry grass appears drought-damaged, but a close inspection may reveal an army of aphids, especially on turf under shade trees.

Control: Aphids are easily controlled with a liquid insecticide labelled for aphids. Insecticidal soap is also effective in controlling these tender pests. Natural predators include ladybugs, lacewings, syrphid flies, and assassin bugs.

3. armyworms

Profile: Yellowish- or brownish-green 1–2-inch-long caterpillars.

Damage: Often attacking in large numbers, maneuvering at night, they devour leaves and stems of grass. If not controlled immediately, they can destroy large sections of lawn overnight.

Control: Use a granular or liquid insecticide to control these surface feeders early in their life cycle.

4. billbugs

Profile: Adult weevils are about $\frac{1}{2}$ inch long, dark brown to black, with a curved snout. Larvae are small, $\frac{1}{8}$- to $\frac{1}{4}$-inch legless white grubs with brown heads.

Damage: Adult weevils eat holes in Kentucky bluegrass and other cool-season grasses. After hatching, billbug larvae feed on the grass blade crowns, then move into the soil and feed on roots.

Control: They are easiest to kill in their adult weevil stage before they lay eggs. Look for adults in late spring and apply an insecticide labeled effective against billbugs.

5. chinch bugs

Profile: Pinkish-red insects with cream-colored bands around midsection when nymphs first hatch. Adults are black to brown, $\frac{1}{5}$-inch-long bugs with white wings.

Damage: Feed on grass in full sun, avoiding shady areas. Prefer St. Augustinegrass, causing yellowish patches that eventually turn brown and die.

Control: Apply a granular or liquid insecticide labeled for chinch bug control and look for varieties of St. Augustinegrass, such as 'Floralawn' or 'Floratam,' which resist this pest.

6. cutworms

Profile: Similar to sod webworms, these 2-inch-long black or brown caterpillars are moth larvae. Often found in spring and summer curled into a C shape in thatch near the lawn surface.

Damage: Emerge at night to eat vegetables, flowers, grass, and just about any other vegetation. Affected lawns will have small brown patches.

Control: Granular or spray insecticides applied in evening are effective.

7. bermudagrass mites

Profile: These tiny eight-legged pests are spider-related arachnids.

Damage: Bermudagrass mites have a particular taste for this turf. While sucking the juices of leaves and stems, they inject a toxin that causes the grass to grow in stubby, distorted witches' brooms that turn yellow and then die.

Control: Buy modern Bermudagrass hybrids resistant to mites. If you have mites, mow low, discard clippings, and apply a miticide labeled for control of Bermudagrass mite.

8. mole crickets

Profile: Some of the ugliest pests in existence, these large, 1-inch pests burrow in lawns throughout the Southeast.

Damage: They feed on roots, stems, and grass blades, burrowing large tunnels and building small soil mounds as they claw their way around the lawn.

Control: Aerate to prevent thatch. Grub controls are effective when applied in early summer. Insecticides must be watered in.

9. sod webworms

Profile: Inch-long smooth, green, or light brown caterpillars with rows of spots. Adults are $\frac{3}{4}$-inch tan moths with beaklike mouths that fly out of the lawn when disturbed.

Damage: Caterpillars build web-lined tunnels in the lawn and feed on grass blades, causing scalped, yellowish-brown patches that worsen during droughts.

Control: Sod webworms are surface feeders so they are easy to control with a contact granular or liquid insecticide applied in the evening.

10. white grubs

Profile: The larval stage of several species of beetles including Japanese beetles, June bugs, and chafers.

Damage: Feed on roots, killing the turf. May also lead to an increase in damage from moles, raccoons, and other nuisance critters that consider grubs a delicacy. Pull back the dead turf in summer and look for these C-shape white worms.

Control: Grubs are a common problem, so a number of insecticides are designated specifically for them. Best applied in spring or early summer, insecticides help control larvae as they hatch from eggs.

the importance of fertilizer

Some lawn owners withhold fertilizer in hopes that not applying it will mean less mowing. The reality is that a nutrient-starved lawn will ultimately mean more maintenance because a weak lawn needs more herbicides and more mowing to keep down the fast-growing weeds. Fertilizer does more than make grass grow quickly and give it a dark green color. It contributes to the overall health of the grass plant.

Proper fertilization is one of the best things you can do to maintain a healthy lawn, and it's fairly simple. In the past, chemical fertilizer products contained only quick-release nitrogen that caused sudden growth spurts. If people miscalculated their application rate, they burned their lawn to a crisp. Modern lawn fertilizers offer slow-release nitrogen to provide an extended meal for your lawn. This helps prevent fertilizer burn and avoids the feast-or-famine scenario.

Setting up an annual lawn care program is the key to helping a lawn grow its best. Following a program is like keeping your car operating at peak performance by adhering to the maintenance schedule prescribed in the owner's manual.

An annual lawn care program takes into consideration the fertilizer requirements of the lawn and anticipates seasonal problems, such as weeds or grubs, that the lawn will likely face. Then it sets up a calendar for applying control materials and fertilizer. With an annual program, you're sure to put down the right product at the right time to eliminate problems, as well as build the thickness, density, and health of the turf.

To determine how much fertilizer you'll need, start by figuring the square footage of your lawn. See "Figure Your Footage" (below left). Once you know how large your lawn is, you can determine how much fertilizer to buy by reading the coverage on the label.

timing of lawn fertilizer

When you fertilize and the number of applications you'll need depends on the length of your growing season. Grass in warmer zones with longer growing seasons will need more applications than the same variety of grass in a cooler region with shorter summers. Heavy-feeding, warm-season grasses such as Bermudagrass, zoysiagrass, and St. Augustinegrass benefit from applications in early spring, early summer, late summer, and early fall. Cool-season grasses such as Kentucky bluegrass and fescue are more active in spring and fall, so they prefer applications in spring, and a light application in summer followed by heavier

figure your footage

When it comes to calculating the amount of fertilizer (as well as other products) to apply to your lawn, you need to know your square footage. Not every lawn is a perfect square, so here's how to figure the area of common shapes. If you have a free-form lawn, think of it as a combination of different shapes; measure those different shapes and total their amounts for square footage.

Square or rectangle	Area = L × W L = length W = width
Triangle	Area = 0.5 × B × H B = base H = height
Circle	Area = πr² π = 3.14 r² = radius, squared

applications in late summer and fall. Fortunately, you are not on your own when it comes to preparing an annual schedule for your lawn. The better brands of lawn products generally include recommendations of when and how to apply the product as part of the directions. The *Scotts Lawns* book contains detailed charts outlining lawn fertilization programs for various regions of North America.

The best time of day to fertilize your lawn is early morning. Less wind means the fine particles won't blow around and the morning dew helps the fertilizer stay put on the lawn. This is particularly important for weed-and-feed products that need contact time to act on the weeds. Follow irrigation directions on the bag for washing fertilizer pellets off the blades of grass and into the soil since these directions vary depending on the product.

the three components of fertilizer

Fertilizers often contain many elements, but the three most important are nitrogen, phosphorous, and potassium. These elements, in that order, are represented by the numbers on fertilizer labels. As a rule, lawn fertilizers are high in nitrogen because it's the element grasses need most. So, you are likely to see a formula such as 30-3-4 on lawn fertilizer, meaning the contents of the bag by weight are 30 percent nitrogen (N), 3 percent phosphorous (P_2O_5), and 4 percent potassium (K_2O). If a fertilizer is 30 percent nitrogen, you would need to apply only 3.3 pounds of it per application on 1,000 square feet of lawn to provide the same feeding as 100 pounds of fertilizer with 1 percent nitrogen—not very practical.

reading a fertilizer label
Here is a breakdown of why these elements are needed. There's an easy way to remember it: N—up (blades), P—down (roots), and K—all around (general vigor).

N

Nitrogen boosts growth and gives grass blades that rich verdant color. Lawn fertilizers are high in nitrogen.

P

Phosphorous helps build strong roots and is important for young seedlings.

K

Potassium gives grass general vigor, strengthening its resistance to drought, cold, and disease.

Annual lawn care programs are cyclical with no defined beginning or end. You can start anywhere in the cycle and from there move on to successive points.

spreading fertilizer

If you plan ahead a little, your fertilizing will go much more smoothly. Get up bright and early, before the wind kicks up and when dew is still on the grass. The dew will help you keep track of your progress, but if no dew is present, be careful you do not confuse spreader wheel tracks with the tracks made by the mower earlier.

You'll need some type of spreader to distribute fertilizer properly. Selecting the right model depends mainly on the size of your lawn (see "Selecting a Spreader" on the opposite page). The key is to spread the fertilizer evenly. Don't try to do this by hand, even if you have a small lawn. No matter what type of spreader you have, you need to figure out how to set the distribution rate. You can usually find the information you need on the fertilizer bag or in the spreader instructions. If not, check the bag or search the Internet to locate the spreader manufacturer and contact their technical support staff.

To avoid burning your lawn with fertilizer spills, always rest your spreader on a hard surface before you begin filling it. Keep in mind that spreaders are calibrated with the assumption that the person behind the controls is walking at a normal pace. If you streak across the yard like you're running a 50-yard dash or poke along at a snail's pace, it will affect the rate of application. You can decrease the rate of application a fraction to adjust for an unavoidably slow gait. Start by creating header strips by making a lap or two around the edges. This will give more precise control around the edges and allow room to maneuver at the ends after you start walking in rows. Walk the yard lengthwise so that you make fewer turns. Close the hopper as you reach the header strip at the end of each row or whenever you are turning. Don't reopen it until you start walking the next strip.

When the job is done, sweep up any fertilizer on walkways, driveways, streets, and other paved areas. This will prevent stains and keep fertilizer out of storm drains. Rinse your spreader thoroughly with a strong stream of water. Allow it to dry thoroughly and give any metal parts, including the axle, a coat of a cleaner or lubricant such as WD-40 before putting it into storage. Check the fertilizer label to see if you need to water after application. If so, turn on the sprinklers to water the nutrients into the soil and kick back and watch the grass grow.

▼ This fertilizer spreader offers the advantage of precision placement of fertilizer for tight spots or near flower beds switching to broadcast mode to cover open ground fast.

◀◀ Adjust the fertilizer spreader setting according to the directions on the product you purchase.

◀ Drinking and fertilizer spreading don't mix. With drop spreaders, it's particularly important to avoid gaps in application for uniform results.

◣ Fertilize early in the morning when dew still blankets the lawn and prior to mowing. This will make it easier to follow the depressions made by the wheels.

◀ Broadcast spreaders are best for wide open areas where they won't throw lawn fertilizer onto nearby flower beds or landscaped areas.

selecting a spreader
Four basic types of fertilizer spreaders exist, each with its own advantages and disadvantages.

Handheld crank spreader
These hold only a few pounds of fertilizer, so they are suitable only for small lawns. They can be tiring to hold for long periods and difficult to coordinate. And it's often difficult to find a fertilizer that offers recommended settings for a handheld spreader.

Drop spreader
This type of spreader dispenses fertilizer by dropping it gently out of the bottom of the hopper. Drop spreaders work well when you need to avoid spreading an herbicide or fertilizer onto adjacent areas. It's important to overlap the wheel tracks just a few inches to avoid the striping effect caused by too much overlap or gaps that receive no fertilizer.

Broadcast spreader
Also called rotary spreaders, these models cover a strip 4–8 feet wide, so they work well for large lawns. Some models are designed to be pulled by a lawn tractor for even faster coverage. Because they fling fertilizer in a semicircle, it's difficult to apply it accurately, so you may end up with pellets in nearby planting beds.

Combination spreader
This recent invention offers the best of both worlds. It covers ground as quickly as a broadcast spreader but also offers the option of an edge guard that can be activated to prevent wasting fertilizer along driveways and other hard surfaces or flinging it into planting beds.

▲ Don't guess at the amount of fertilizer to apply to trees, shrubs, and perennials. Follow label instructions and measure carefully before applying.

maintaining the rest of your lawnscape

fertilizing landscape plants

Fertilizing the trees, shrubs, perennials, and annuals around your landscape is a bit more complicated than fertilizing the lawn. A glance at the overwhelming variety of fertilizers at your local garden center can be intimidating. A basic understanding of the types of fertilizer available will help you make the right choice for you and your plants.

Most fertilizers are dry, granular products containing some percentage of the three key elements—nitrogen, phosphorous, and potassium. Moisture and heat dissolve them and release the nutrients into the soil so that roots can absorb them. As with lawn fertilizer, look for a fertilizer with slow-release nitrogen that will feed your plants over time. Nitrogen moves through the soil quickly, but phosphorous and potassium move much slower and will not be readily available to roots if the fertilizer is just sprinkled atop soil around your plants. If you can, mix fertilizers into the soil when you are preparing the bed so that the nutrients are at root level. For established plants, add the recommended amount of fertilizer around the drip line.

A hand cultivator won't get nutrients deep enough for trees and large shrubs. One convenient option is to use fertilizer spikes, which are compressed tubes of fertilizers that can be hammered into the ground. You can do the same thing by hammering a metal spike or pipe 6 inches or so into the ground, removing it, and then filling the hole with a granular fertilizer labeled for trees and shrubs. Be careful to follow the recommended rate for the size of your tree or shrub. A funnel placed in the hole will help get fertilizer down into the ground without burning the lawn or surrounding plants.

Liquid fertilizers and water-soluble fertilizers offer quick relief to plants needing a boost. These fast-release nitrogen formulas work well for vegetables, houseplants, and container plants. The disadvantage of their solubility is that the nutrients must be replenished often—every two weeks or so during the growing season.

coming to terms

Here are explanations for some of the terms you'll see on fertilizer labels:

acidifying fertilizers—Sometimes marketed as azalea, camellia, or rhododendron food, these fertilizers produce acids as they decompose. Nearly all chemical fertilizers produce some acid, but these are stronger. If you notice the leaves of azaleas or other acidlovers turning yellow, it can be a sign that the soil is too alkaline and could benefit from a shot of an acidifying fertilizer. If a soil sample indicates you have alkaline soil, you should use acidifying fertilizers on all plants.

bloom boosters—Often marketed as fertilizers for annuals, these fertilizers generally have a high middle number, such as 10-52-10, because they are loaded with phosphorus, an important element in bloom production.

foliar fertilizers—These water-soluble fertilizers can be absorbed through the leaves of a plant.

incomplete fertilizers—One step up from a simple fertilizer, incomplete fertilizers contain just two of the three main elements, N-P-K.

micronutrients—Also called trace elements, these are needed by plants in small amounts. After the N-P-K amounts are listed on the label of a fertilizer, the fine print will list percentages of manganese (Mn), sulfur (S), iron (Fe), and other micronutrients.

organic fertilizers—There is much debate over what officially qualifies as "organic," but it generally means the product is derived solely from the remains of organisms that were once living or it is a byproduct of a living organism. Organic fertilizers rely on organisms in the soil to release the nutrients, generally over a long period. Hundreds of organic products are available, including bat guano, blood meal, bone meal, cottonseed meal, fish emulsion, earthworm castings, treated sewage sludge, and a variety of manures from many different mammals. Organic products are good for improving soil structure and encouraging beneficial microorganisms in the soil.

simple fertilizers—Fertilizers that contain just one of the three key nutrients, usually nitrogen in the form of ammonium sulfate (21-0-0).

▲ Water-soluble fertilizers feed plants two ways: through the leaves and through the roots. Use them every 7-14 days.

▲ A liquid starter fertilizer will reduce stress from being planted (or transplanted) and promote root growth to get new plants off to a quick start.

▲ Whether in containers or in the ground, flowers and vegetables need nutrients. With this slow-release feeder, you only have to feed once every three months.

▲ Fertilizer spikes are a convenient way to get slow-release nutrients down to root level. Use the spikes once per season.

▲ Mulch touching the base of trees and shrubs should be ½-inch thick or less. You can lay it on thicker (4 to 6 inches) farther from the trunk.

the joys of mulch

Whether it's grass clippings on the lawn or shredded bark on the planting beds, mulch is a good thing. It retains moisture, reduces soil compaction, holds back weeds, insulates the soil from temperature extremes, contributes to soil structure as it decomposes, and makes your landscape look tidy.

There is such a thing as too much of a good thing, however. If you replenish mulch faster than the mulch can break down, you end up with a thick blanket that will smother plant roots, depriving them of oxygen and water. For most mulches, a layer 2 to 4 inches thick is ideal. However, a fluffy layer of pine straw or salt marsh hay can be slightly thicker, and a mat-forming layer of grass clippings should be only 1 or 2 inches thick. Never pile mulch against the trunks of trees and shrubs. Every mulch has idiosyncrasies, so get to know your mulch before piling it on (see "Mulch at a Glance," opposite page).

On your lawn, mulch comes from the clippings that your mower spits out. Grass clippings don't contribute to a thatch problem as long as you mow regularly and remove no more than one-third of the grass blade at a time. Clippings will settle to help prevent weeds, hold in moisture, and contribute organic matter, nitrogen, and other nutrients to your soil. If you have gone too long between mowings and need to bag your clippings, deposit them in a compost pile or sprinkle them in planting beds. If you have applied an herbicide to your lawn, don't use the clippings around your herb or vegetable garden.

▼ It's OK to have a little mulch visible to separate and highlight colorful plants such as the sedum, Russian sage, and rosemary seen here.

mulch at a glance

Each mulch has a slightly different appearance, benefit, and drawback. Here are the pros and cons of some popular choices.

Mulch	Positives	Drawbacks
Shredded bark	Attractive. Widely available in bags and bulk. Holds to slopes better than bark chips. Long-lasting; cypress mulch lasts longer than pine or other hardwoods.	Few drawbacks.
Pine straw	Popular in the southeastern U.S., where pines are abundant. It's renewable, easily transported in bales, ideal for slopes, and attractive. Good choice for acid-loving plants.	Attractive reddish color fades quickly. Deteriorates quickly and needs replenishing twice a year. The light weight makes it a bad choice for windy areas.
Grass clippings	Abundant and free. Clippings are mostly water, so they decompose quickly, returning nutrients to the soil. Widely available in bags and bulk.	Form a moldy, smelly mat if applied too thickly; 2 inches is sufficient. Herbicides that were applied to the lawn can harm mulched plants.
Bark chips	Widely available in bags and bulk. Attractive.	Wash away on slopes and low areas. Unless colored chips are used, turn an unattractive gray color as they weather; large chips look worse than small ones.
Cocoa hulls	Smell like chocolate cake for several weeks after being applied. Attractive dark brown color. Provide potassium and other nutrients for plants.	Can get moldy if they remain wet for long periods. They're also expensive; sold by the bag, rarely in bulk.
Shredded leaves	Free and widely available. Renewable resource. Improve soil structure as they decay. Shredded leaves stay in place and allow water to penetrate better than whole leaves.	Not the most attractive option. Most decompose quickly, so you need to replenish often.
Sawdust	Inexpensive if you have a sawmill nearby. Easy to apply.	Robs nitrogen from soil if not composted first. Can blow or wash away easily. Rarely sold in bags, only bulk.
Hardwood mulch	Widely available. Inexpensive or free.	May attract insects. Hosts fungal problems. Robs nitrogen from soil if not composted first.

Pine straw

Shredded pine bark

Small pine bark

Hardwood mulch

Cypress mulch

Cocoa hulls

pruning trees and shrubs

Prune the trees and shrubs in your landscape for three basic reasons—safety, the health of the plant, and aesthetics. When done correctly, the result is a hazard-free landscape with attractive, healthy plants. When done incorrectly, pruning can have just the opposite result.

Start pruning trees and shrubs while they are still young. This will set the stage for a well-grown tree that won't require expensive remedial pruning when it is large. For large trees and pruning involving utility lines or other risky situations, call in a professional.

A good, clean cut is critical to ensure the health of your plant and the safety of everyone who enters your landscape. If the cut is rough or leaves torn bark or an ugly stub, the plant won't form a callus quickly and heal properly. The longer a wound is open, the more susceptible it is to pests. If you suspect that parts of the plant are diseased, sterilize your pruners after each cut with alcohol or bleach. Pruning stems just above a bud stimulates it and the buds below to grow. If the cut is made more than $1/4$ inch above the bud, this leaves a stub that dies and invites insects and disease. Pruning too close can damage the bud below and cause the same problems.

Remove branches that rub together or grow at an awkward angle. Prune out branches that rub against buildings and other structures. If repeated pruning is needed to keep a plant off your home or other structure, this is a sign that it was planted in the wrong place, and you should consider transplanting it or removing it. If a plant has two central leaders or a Y-crotch, remove the weaker branch. If not, the tree will likely split down the center in the future. Water sprouts, clusters of

the right tools

The right tool will make pruning easier and produce a better cut that heals faster. To extend the life of tools and make better cuts, maintain a sharp edge by sharpening and keep tools clean and well-oiled.

- **Shears**—Also called hedge clippers, these are used for snipping soft tissue and twigs less than $1/8$ inch in diameter. Because they are used to make numerous cuts in rapid succession, shears dull quickly.

- **Hand pruners**—Two basic types are available—anvil and bypass. The anvil type often bruises one side of the stem you're cutting. Bypass pruners use a curved blade to slice against an edge for a clean cut. Good sharp hand pruners should cut through most green wood up to $1/2$ inch in diameter.

- **Loppers**—These long-handled pruners offer better leverage for pruning branches from $1/2$ to 1 inch thick. They also offer a longer reach, which can be handy for reaching into thick or thorny shrubs.

- **Pruning saw**—Use a pruning saw for branches 1 inch to 4 inches in diameter. A curved blade and large, jagged teeth make quick work of removing large branches. Look for a model that offers replacement blades.

- **Pole pruner**—This tool does the work of lopping shears and a pruning saw, with the added benefit of a long handle. The blade is controlled by a length of rope, allowing your feet to remain on the ground while you cut branches high overhead.

Hand pruners

Loppers

twigs that sometimes emerge near old cuts, should also be removed. Remove any suckers that emerge at the base of a tree. Most shrubs are best pruned into a vase shape that opens up the center for better sun exposure and air circulation.

Pruning for aesthetics is in the eye of the beholder. It can be as fanciful as creating topiary animals or as precise as training a bonsai. You may want to brighten your landscape by limbing up a large shade tree or tidying up a shaggy shrub. Pruning can also improve flowering. Deadheading spent blooms encourages repeat blooming throughout the growing season. If pruning is timed right, you can also encourage more blooms the next year.

When to prune depends on where you live and the individual plant, but a few general guidelines apply. Prune spring-blooming plants right after they finish flowering, before they set buds for the following year. While it won't harm them to prune in early spring, you will decrease the number of blooms that year. Summer-blooming plants should be pruned in late winter. Most deciduous trees and shrubs respond well to dormant pruning in winter. Birches and maples lose a lot of sap when pruned in late winter, so many people wait until summer to prune them. Avoid pruning oak trees from April 15 to July 1, when insects that spread oak wilt are most active. Evergreens are best pruned in early summer, after the new growth is obvious. Discontinue pruning all plants from late summer through early fall. Pruning at the end of the growing season stimulates tender new growth that doesn't have time to harden off before the first winter freeze.

three-step pruning of trees

Large tree branches should be pruned using a three-step process to avoid stripping the bark from the tree trunk as the branch falls away.

step 1. Using a pruning saw, make a shallow cut through the bark on the underside of the branch several inches from the trunk.

step 2. Starting at the top side of the branch and a few inches farther out than your undercut, cut all the way through the branch.

step 3. Make a final clean cut to remove the stub. Make this cut just outside the branch collar, the swollen area where the branch joins the trunk.

pruning overgrown shrubs

Renovating an old shrub will improve its health and beauty. A good approach is to remove one-third of the limbs each year for three years. The best time for this task is late winter or early spring so that plants can recover before the summer heat zaps their energy.

stage 1. The first year, prune the oldest, most damaged limbs to within 4 to 6 inches of the ground.

stage 2. The second year, remove one-third of the oldest limbs.

stage 3. When one-third of the limbs are pruned in the third year, you have an invigorated new plant rather than an unsightly stump.

resources

For more information about lawn care or the tools featured in this book, consult these resources.

information

Better Homes and Gardens
www.bhg.com
Garden discussion groups.
Garden plans.
Garden questions and answers.
Garden slide shows.
Plant finder.
Regional garden tips.
Zone maps.

The Mole Man
www.themoleman.com
All about how to trap moles.

Miracle-Gro
www.MiracleGro.com
Free e-mail gardening reminders.
Video quick tips.
Weed finder.

Ortho
www.ortho.com
Bug finder.
Weed finder.
Ortho Problem Solver on line.
Free e-mail gardening tips.

The Scotts Company
www.scotts.com
14111 Scottslawn Rd.
Marysville, OH 43041
800/543-TURF
Annual program builder.
Identify your grass.
Lawn products calculator.
E-mail gardening reminder.
Project tips.

Weather.com
www.weather.com/gardening/maps/
palmer__drought__720x486.html
Drought information updated daily.

universities

Colorado State University
www.colostate.edu/Depts/bspm/
Internet sites on entomology.

Delaware Cooperative Extension
www.bluehen.ags.udel.edu/deces/pp/
pp-06.htm
Lawn disease identification.

Iowa State University
www.ent.iastate.edu/imagegallery/
default.html
Insect image gallery.

www.hort.iastate.edu/pages/conshort/
c__frame.html
Various topics for consumers on
gardening, lawn care, and pesticide use.

Mississippi State University
www.msucares.com/lawn/lawn__diseases
Lawn diseases.

Ohio State University
plantfacts.ohio-state.edu/
Fact sheet database.

www.bugs.osu.edu/~bugdoc/Shetlar/
factsheet/index.htm
Insect fact sheets .

Purdue University
www.agry.purdue.edu/turf/tips/index.html
Turf tips.

Rutgers University
www.rce.rutgers.edu/weeds/index.html
Various pictures on many weeds.

University of Georgia
www.ces.uga.edu
Various horticultural topics.

University of Illinois
www.life.uiuc.edu/entomology/
resourceindex.html
Pictures of various insects.

www.urbanext.uiuc.edu/lawntalk
Questions & answers on lawns.

University of Kentucky
www.uky.edu/Agriculture/Entomology/
entfacts/efpdflst.htm
Entomology fact sheets.

Virginia Tech
www.ppws.vt.edu/weedindex.htm
Alphabetical index listing of weeds.

USDA plant hardiness zone maps

This map of climate zones helps you select plants for your garden that will survive a typical winter in your region. The United States Department of Agriculture (USDA) developed the map, basing the zones on the lowest recorded temperatures across North America. Zone 1 is the coldest area and Zone 11 is the warmest.

Plants are classified by the coldest temperature and zone they can endure. For example, plants hardy to Zone 6 survive where winter temperatures drop to −10° F. Those hardy to Zone 8 die long before it's that

cold. These plants may grow in colder regions but must be replaced each year. Plants rated for a range of hardiness zones can usually survive winter in the coldest region as well as tolerate the summer heat of the warmest one.

To find your hardiness zone, note the approximate location of your community on the map, then match the color band marking that area to the key.

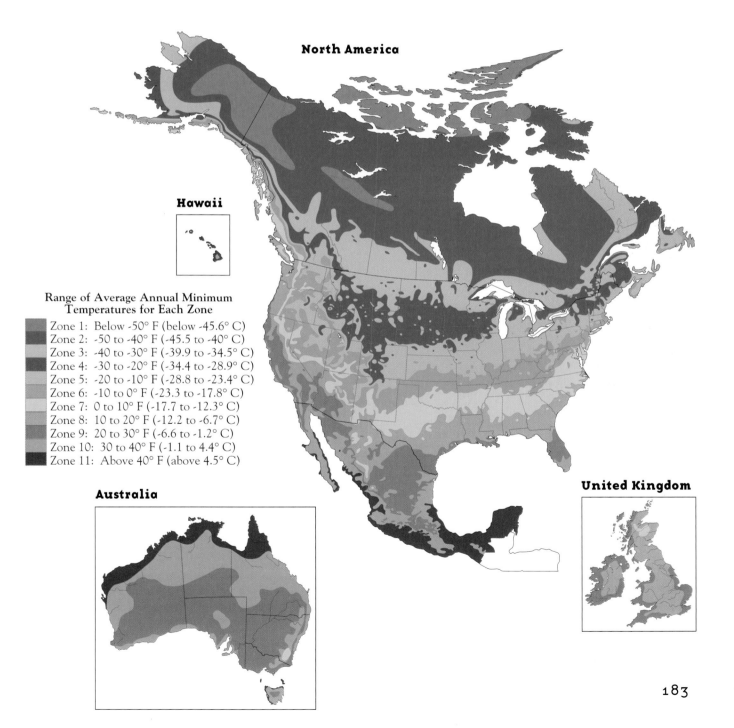

North America

Hawaii

Range of Average Annual Minimum Temperatures for Each Zone

Zone 1: Below -50° F (below -45.6° C)
Zone 2: -50 to -40° F (-45.5 to -40° C)
Zone 3: -40 to -30° F (-39.9 to -34.5° C)
Zone 4: -30 to -20° F (-34.4 to -28.9° C)
Zone 5: -20 to -10° F (-28.8 to -23.4° C)
Zone 6: -10 to 0° F (-23.3 to -17.8° C)
Zone 7: 0 to 10° F (-17.7 to -12.3° C)
Zone 8: 10 to 20° F (-12.2 to -6.7° C)
Zone 9: 20 to 30° F (-6.6 to -1.2° C)
Zone 10: 30 to 40° F (-1.1 to 4.4° C)
Zone 11: Above 40° F (above 4.5° C)

Australia

United Kingdom

index

Page numbers in **bold** type indicate illustrations.

Thanks to
Cathy Wilkinson Barash, DripWorks, Hound Dog Products, Inc., Mary Irene Swartz

Photographers
(Photographers credited may retain copyright © to the listed photographs.)
L = Left, R = Right, C = Center, B = Bottom, T = Top

William D. Adams: 133B; **Liz Ball/Positive Images:** 131CBL; **Cathy Wilkinson Barash:** 47CL, 156, 165TR; **Mark Bolton/Garden Picture Library:** 111TL, 150Row4#2; **Lynne Brotchie/Garden Picture Library:** 21L; **Patricia Bruno/Positive Images:** 133T, 139B; **Gay Bumgarner/Positive Images:** 126; **Karen Bussolini/Positive Images:** 97BC; **Brian Carter/Garden Picture Library:** 95R; **Walter Chandoha:** 21R, 98TL; **Nick Christians:** 170#6; **Crandall & Crandall:** 36, 80L, 81R, 133CR, 160CR, 161, 162R; **Eric Crichton/Garden Picture Library:** 66, 76BR, 91BR; **R. Todd Davis:** 53T, 59BL, 150Row1#2, 150Row1#3, 150Row4#1, 153B; **Catriona Tudor Erler:** 8, 12T, 12B, 15T, 20, 31, 51TL, 53B, 54T, 59BR, 76TL, 78B, 82T, 83TR, 86, 88B, 90, 92TR, 105BL, 105BR, 107T, 116T, 122TL, 144T, 149T, 150Row2#1; **Ron Evans/Garden Picture Library:** 103R; **Derek Fell:** 40, 93B; **Christopher Gallagher/Garden Picture Library:** 102B, 166R; **John Glover:** 75, 107B, 155T; **John Glover/Garden Picture Library:** 5C, 11BL, 91TR, 135B, 178B; **Jerry Harpur:** 4C, 18TR (Switzerland. Balconies in Geneva),

18BL (Arabella Lennox Boyd), 18BR (Design: Jill Billington, RHS Chelsea 1991), 51R (Stellenberg), 54BL (Frances Shannon), 56B (Alfaro, Madrid), 58 (Alfaro, Madrid), 61TL (RHS Chelsea), 61B (Simon Fraser), 68 (Christopher Masson), 76TR (Old Rectory, Burghfield), 76BL (Kettle Hill), 88TL (John & Penny Zino, Flaxmere New Zealand), 89TL (Yeomana Tadmarton Garden), 89TR (Nick & Pam Coote, Oxford), 93BC (Patricia Larson, Boston), 94L, 97C (Cottesbrooke), 97BR (Pam Armour), 101TL (Oehme Van Sweden), 103L (Saling Hall), 113 (Richard Shelbourne), 114B (Jean Anderson), 145B (Linda Cochran); **Hound Dog Products, Inc.:** 137BR; **Jerry Howard/Positive Images:** 30, 49BL, 64T, 147T, 150Row3#4; **Roger Hyam/Garden Picture Library:** 84; **Bill Johnson:** 101BR; **Wolfgang Kaehler:** 4TL, 11TL, 11CL, 12C; **Jim Kalisch:** 170#3; **Larry Kassell:** 43B, 134; **Rosemary Kautzky:** 105T, 116B, 131TL, 149BL, 149BC, 149BR, 166L, 181B; **Lamontagne/Garden Picture Library:** 95L, 160BR, 179#3; **Michael Landis:** 168#6; **Andrew Lawson:** 2 (Designer: Wendy Lauderdale), 43TL, 87 (Penelope Hobhouse), 98TR (Anthony Noel), 102T, 150Row2#2; **Levittown Historical Society:** 15CL; **Library of Congress:** 10, 11BR; **David Liebman:** 170#8; **Charles Mann:** 127T; **Kathy Mansfield/Positive Images:** 89B; **Marilynn McAra:** 5TL, 98C (Designer/Gardener: Binh Huy Duong); **Clive Nichols:** 17 (Designer: Penny Smith), 49TL (Sarah Layton); **Clive Nochols/Garden Picture Library:** 92BR, 93T, 97BL (Anthony Noel), 101TR; **Geoffrey Nilsen:** 69BL;

Philip L. Nixon: 170#2; **Jerry Pavia:** 19, 51CL, 54BR, 59TL, 98B, 101BL, 150Row2#3, 152L, 153T; **Rain Bird Corporation:** 119BL, 119#1R, 119#7R, 124; **Cheryl R. Richter:** 14, 155B; **The Scotts Company:** 111BR, 131BL, 131BC, 131BR, 167CL, 167CR, 167R, 168#1, 168#4, 168#7, 168#8, 168#9, 173BL, 173BCL, 173BCR, 173BR, 173CR, 177L, 177LC, 177RC, 177R; **Lynn Seldon:** 83TL; **Richard Shiell:** 69BR, 70TL, 92TL, 93TC, 145T, 150Row2#4, 150Row4#3, 150Row4#4, 154, 160BL, 168#3; **Neil Soderstrom:** 110TL, 110TR, 122TR, 125T, 181TL, 181TC, 181TR; **Pam Spaulding/Positive Images:** 88TR; **Joseph G. Strauch, Jr.:** 150Row1#1, 175TR; **Graham Strong/Garden Picture Library:** 92BL; **Ron Sutherland/Garden Picture Library:** 61TR; **Brigitte Thomas/Garden Picture Library:** 74R, 114TR; **Michael S. Thompson:** 16, 18TL, 22, 26T, 47CR, 47BL. 47BR, 83B, 91L, 92CL, 97T, 106, 108, 111TR, 115B, 115T, 119TL, 127B, 139T, 140, 140T, 149C, 150Row1#4, 150Row3#1, 150Row3#3, 158, 162L, 179#1, 179#2, 179#4, 180R; **Rob van Nostrand:** 170#1; **Juliette Wade/Garden Picture Library:** 62TR; **Tom Watschke:** 168#10; **Mel Watson/Gaden Picture Library:** 121TL; **Mary Howell-Williams:** 150Row3#2; **Justyn Willsmore:** 5BL, 43CL, 94BR, 100, 110CL, 110CR, 121BL, 137BL, 162C; **Steven Wooster/Garden Picture Library:** 6, 147B; **Gayle Worf:** 168#5; **Kate Zari Roberts/Garden Picture Library:** 94TR

Scotts Lawnscaping
Editor: Denny Schrock
Writer: Glenn R. DiNella
Contributing Editor: Lynn Steiner
Assistant Editor: Harijs Priekulis
Copy Chief: Terri Fredrickson
Copy and Production Editor: Victoria Forlini
Photographers: Marty Baldwin, Scott Little, Jay Wilde
Editorial Operations Manager: Karen Schirm
Managers, Book Production: Pam Kvitne,
    Marjorie J. Schenkelberg, Rick von Holdt
Contributing Copy Editor: Sharon McHaney
Technical Proofreaders: Nick Christians, Ashton Ritchie,
    Paul C. Siciliano, Jr.
Contributing Proofreaders: Mark John Conley, Pamela
    Elizian, Heidi Johnson
Contributing Illustrator: Tom Rosborough
Contributing Map Illustrator: Jana Fothergill
Contributing Prop/Photo Stylist: Susan Strelecki
Indexer: Ann Truesdale
Electronic Production Coordinator: Paula Forest
Editorial and Design Assistants: Kathleen Stevens,
    Karen McFadden

**Additional Editorial Contributions from
    Neymeyer Photo/Design**
Director: Lyne Neymeyer

Meredith® Books
Editor in Chief: Linda Raglan Cunningham
Design Director: Matt Strelecki
Executive Editor, Gardening and Home Improvement:
    Benjamin W. Allen
Executive Editor, Gardening: Michael McKinley

Publisher: James D. Blume
Executive Director, Marketing: Jeffrey Myers
Executive Director, New Business Development:
    Todd M. Davis
Executive Director, Sales: Ken Zagor
Director, Operations: George A. Susral
Director, Production: Douglas M. Johnston
Business Director: Jim Leonard

Vice President and General Manager: Douglas J. Guendel

Meredith Publishing Group
President, Publishing Group: Stephen M. Lacy
Vice President-Publishing Director: Bob Mate

Meredith Corporation
Chairman and Chief Executive Officer: William T. Kerr
In Memoriam: E.T. Meredith III (1933-2003)

Note to the Readers: Due to differing conditions, tools, and individual skills, Meredith Corporation assumes no responsibility for any damages, injuries suffered, or losses incurred as a result of following the information published in this book. Before beginning any project, review the instructions carefully, and if any doubts or questions remain, consult local experts or authorities. Because codes and regulations vary greatly, you always should check with authorities to ensure that your project complies with all applicable local codes and regulations. Always read and observe all of the safety precautions provided by manufacturers of any tools, equipment, or supplies, and follow all accepted safety procedures.

All of us at Meredith® Books are dedicated to providing you with the information and ideas you need to enhance your home and garden. We welcome your comments and suggestions about this book. Write to us at:

Meredith Corporation
Meredith Gardening Books
1716 Locust St.
Des Moines, IA 50309–3023

If you would like to purchase any of our gardening, home improvement, cooking, crafts, or home decorating and design books, check wherever quality books are sold. Or visit us at: meredithbooks.com

If you would like more information on other Scotts products, call 800-543-TURF or visit us at: www.Scotts.com